Change Your Life

A Guided Journey Toward Living Your Dream Life

(How to Get More Done With Less Effort and Change Your Life in the Process)

Cary Johnston

Published By **Gautam Kumar**

Cary Johnston

All Rights Reserved

Change Your Life: A Guided Journey Toward Living Your Dream Life (How to Get More Done With Less Effort and Change Your Life in the Process)

ISBN 978-1-7386412-6-0

No part of this guidebook shall be reproduced in any form without permission in writing from the publisher except in the case of brief quotations embodied in critical articles or reviews.

Legal & Disclaimer

The information contained in this book is not designed to replace or take the place of any form of medicine or professional medical advice. The information in this book has been provided for educational & entertainment purposes only.

The information contained in this book has been compiled from sources deemed reliable, and it is accurate to the best of the Author's knowledge; however, the Author cannot guarantee its accuracy and validity and cannot be held liable for any errors or omissions. Changes are periodically made to this book. You must consult your doctor or get professional medical advice before using any of the suggested remedies, techniques, or information in this book.

Upon using the information contained in this book, you agree to hold harmless the Author from and against any damages, costs, and expenses, including any legal fees potentially resulting from the application of any of the information provided by this guide. This disclaimer applies to any damages or injury caused by the use and application, whether directly or indirectly, of any advice or information presented, whether for breach of contract, tort, negligence, personal injury, criminal intent, or under any other cause of action.

You agree to accept all risks of using the information presented inside this book. You need to consult a professional medical practitioner in order to ensure you are both able and healthy enough to participate in this program.

Table Of Contents

Chapter 1: Prepare Your Mind 1

Chapter 2: Put Your Personal Life First 6

Chapter 3: Take Immediate Action 20

Chapter 4: Share Your Modest Victories . 26

Chapter 5: Journalize Your Activities and Achievements 41

Chapter 6: Treat Failure as an Experiment 52

Chapter 7: Self-Complementing and Receiving Them 63

Chapter 8: Charm Your Way towards Success 77

Chapter 9: Mindset Shifts Embracing Growth 85

Chapter 10: Health and Wellness 102

Chapter 11: Personal Growth and Development 120

Chapter 12: Simplifying and Decluttering 131

Chapter 13: Acts of Kindness and Volunteerism 137

Chapter 14: Understanding the Power of the Subconscious Mind 141

Chapter 15: The Influence of the Subconscious Mind on Our Behavior 153

Chapter 16: The Placebo Effect in Healing 165

Chapter 17: Practical Guides for Visualization Exercises 175

Chapter 1: Prepare Your Mind

Develop the behavior of power of will and power of will so one can assist you to make extensive strides in reaching the desires and goals you have were given set for yourself.

You Prepare While Everyone Else Enjoys Playing and Daydreaming

Spend the time different humans are losing on pointless hobbies and daydreaming about a brighter destiny that would in the end come their way starting up your very very own destiny in a manner that is intentional.

Get out a chunk of paper or create a highbrow map and use it to map out a short-term, medium-term, and prolonged-time period plan for every aspect of your lifestyles.

Make a plan outlining the activities that you'll carry out tomorrow, this week, this month, and during the route of the one year to help you get one step closer to accomplishing your targets and goals.

If the sports you interact in on a everyday basis are not bringing you any inside the direction of accomplishing your dreams, then those objectives are, quite simply, slipping similarly and similarly out of your advantage. Planning permits get the ball rolling and focuses your interest at the maximum crucial sports so that you can get you in the direction of carrying out your desires.

You Study While Everyone Else Is Asleep

You stay up one, , or 3 hours later than anyone else at night time time time, otherwise you wake up one, , or 3 hours in advance than absolutely everyone else, and you've got a study the whole lot you want to understand to help you in fast accomplishing your goals and targets. This is performed at the same time as each person else is tucked away in their snug beds at night time time.

Learn many talents consisting of a way to network, how to talk in public, a way to good deal, the manner to promote, a way to promote it your self, how to influence others, or even more.

If you positioned inside the attempt to observe while others are having a pipe dream, you will have the competitive benefit an awesome manner to will can help you pull in advance of the p.C..

The building blocks for each kind of accomplishment may be determined in a single's knowledge.

You Improve Yourself thru Listening to People Whine.

When topics do not move as deliberate, which they genuinely will, simply make the effort to mirror and determine out what you may take a look at from the enjoy.

Spend a while thinking about your beyond actions and how you presently understand the scenario. Additionally, spend a while thinking about new perspectives a remarkable manner to help you in adjusting your sails and overcoming those demanding situations within the future.

You are calm and peaceful, silently questioning and gaining knowledge of out of your evaluations whilst others are grousing about their instances and blaming the outdoor worldwide for his or her problems.

You Believe inside the Face of Others' Skepticism The foundations of the amount of self assure you experience on a every day foundation are built upon the ideals you've got.

While unique humans are thinking their competencies, all you need to do is take some time to take into account in your self, expect that there is a solution, and receive as real with that you can convert some detail that seems not viable right into a truth for your self.

You Raise Concerns While Others Complain

When subjects cross from terrible to worse, humans have a propensity to complain and make excuses at the same time as at the equal time in search of to get others to feel sorry for them and their state of affairs.

You, alternatively, aren't deserving of definitely anyone's pity. You, rather, positioned to your wondering cap as soon as topics start to glide incorrect and immediately begin inquisitively analyzing the entirety that lifestyles throws your way. In element of reality, you may preserve to question topics right as plenty due to the fact the factor at which the solutions you have been seeking out are supplied to you in all of their beauty.

Chapter 2: Put Your Personal Life First

When you placed everyone else for your life earlier than yourself, do you ever find that your decrease once more begins off evolved to damage as a end result? Even even as you might not feel bodily soreness to your again, the mental ache you experience due to constantly placing specific human being's requirements earlier than your own builds up and has a sizeable terrible impact for your well-known health. Instead, you need to prioritize looking after yourself specifically else.

When you prioritize looking after yourself, you deliver the area the satisfactory version of who you are and characteristic greater strength to spare at the same time as the possibility to help others affords itself. In addition, putting your very personal necessities first allows you avoid developing resentment towards extraordinary humans, which, in the long term, can be damaging to the fantastic of your interpersonal connections.

I promise that by the point you end studying this put up, your lower lower back will thank you for taking a harm from the steady bending over backwards for one of a kind human beings because of the fact I have to have proven you a few actual strategies in which you could start setting your self first.

The Importance of looking after yourself

To placed one's very own desires above those of others can also, at the beginning appearance, appear to be a egocentric act. But how in the international are you going to make other human beings glad in case you can't even make your self happy?

The findings of the research lend credence to this assertion, as it emerge as found that growing the significance you region on your self and being type to your self each make a contribution to better degrees of happiness.

When I have become extra more youthful, I used to scratch my head and wonder why I grow to be sad with my life irrespective of the truth that I even have end up so energetic in sports that I believed to have importance. But eventually I came to the notion that being concerned in meaningful activities does not necessarily advise that you are in truth searching after yourself and making your goals referred to. This turn out to be a difficult concept for me to certainly be given in advance than the whole lot.

It also can sound like a cliché, however it's miles essential to take note of the flight attendant's commands every even as you are on the plane and once you get off. The notable manner you are going on the way to maintain other human beings and hold your very very personal life is if you located in your very own oxygen mask earlier than trying to help all and sundry else.

Why trying to make each person satisfied may not get you very a protracted way in lifestyles

We all want to be preferred. When different people revel in you and admire you, it gives you a pleasing feeling.

If, rather, the primary purpose of your life is to satisfaction special human beings and win their approval, you are destined to experience permit down. According to the findings of a study that changed into completed inside the three hundred and sixty five days 2000, a preoccupation with the gratification of others is associated with a sophisticated risk of melancholy and a discounted experience of contentment with one's

I can assume lower lower back to a particular scenario in which I was seeking to make actually certainly one of my in-laws satisfied thru putting my very own requirements aside and providing them with some thing it modified into that they favored. But what ended up occurring end up that I started out out to revel in anger closer to this in-regulation on a subconscious diploma, and as a quit quit result, our dating started out to go through because of this. As quick as I set up wonderful limits, I must experience the tension amongst us easing off, and our relationship began out to flourish as a result.

When you placed your hobby on pleasurable unique humans, you end up fascinating certainly everybody but your self. And when it comes to happiness, you deserve it definitely as a whole lot as those particular people do just as masses as you do.

Here is an entire positioned up on the way to train you the way to avoid being a people-pleaser, which you can examine in case you are inquisitive about studying more about the negative effects of this behavior.

five strategies to prioritize your personal desires and hobby

Start placing those five guidelines into exercise as fast as feasible in case you are prepared to put for your oxygen masks first so that you can ultimately breathe and revel in extra pleasure in lifestyles.

1. Constantly remind your self that you may in no way be capable of satisfy the dreams of every single person.

Take every different look at the assertion. And in vicinity of brushing off it out of hand, take it to coronary coronary heart as a few element you recognize to be actual.

You can do your toughest to make sincerely absolutely everyone satisfied, but because of the reality that absolutely everyone have terrific personalities and wonderful requirements, it isn't viable to succeed in this organization.

Every time I try to prepare a meal for a fixed of my friends, I want to endure in thoughts to examine this piece of advice. Attempting to influence my friends to decide a unmarried restaurant for dinner an super way to satisfy each person's alternatives is like seeking to get people inside the United States to agree on some component having to do with politics.

When it comes all of the manner all of the manner down to it, I'm the one who includes a preference wherein we are going, and there are necessarily going to be one or human beings inside the corporation who're going to bitch approximately it. They usually have the option to now not take part if it's miles any such massive depend for them.

Whether you are trying to parent out wherein you want to go out to dinner or making fundamental options in your lifestyles, actually maintain in mind that you could experience masses much less pressured everyday in case you hold in thoughts that it's miles now not your project in life to make certain that everybody else is glad.

2. Decline offers extra regularly.

There are times while putting your self first calls so one can reply inside the terrible.

I grow to be as soon as the shape of worker that could usually solution yes while asked with the useful resource in their manager, no matter how tough the request have come to be for them. It became important to me that my manager idea especially of me and that I established what it supposed to be a diligent employee.

As a impact of this, I located myself running later hours and giving up my social life at a few degree in the primary few years of my expert profession. And much like clockwork, I started out out to despise my process, to the thing that I might say certain at the same time as all I honestly preferred to do end up say no.

I reached my breaking factor, and as a cease result, I in the end mastered the usage of that honest, two-letter word: no.

After I had accomplished this, I now not felt exhausted, and I began out to take pride inside the paintings that I changed into performing another time.

You are not a terrible human for prioritizing yourself and pronouncing no to distinct human beings's requests. You're sincerely defensive your intellectual health and real electricity just so whilst you do say yes to something, you'll be able to offer it your all and make the most of the possibility.

three. Establish suitable limits and obstacles for your relationships.

When it includes alluring individuals in our lives, we commonly care the maximum about fascinating the ones who're the maximum essential to us in my view. You cannot continuously located aside your very very own desires and allow someone take benefit of your kindness, although it is critical to ensure the dreams of your own family are met inside the relationships you've got. And no matter the fact that this is essential, you cannot constantly located your very personal goals first.

When I become a senior in high university, I had no concept what it intended for a courting to have easy limitations, and my partner at the time end up well aware of this reality. Because he have become so busy, he need to request from me to make him lunch or do his schoolwork due to the reality he knew it might be a huge help to him in the ones conditions.

I changed into a naive teenage woman who became obsessed on the concept of affection, so I did whatever he asked of me. I did the entirety he requested of me. And subsequently, I frequently fell in the again of on my own responsibilities or misplaced friendships due to my procrastination.

When I reflect onconsideration on the options I made on the time, it makes me want to throw up. I did now not set up healthy limitations in that dating, which contributed to its unhealthiness. These boundaries must have emphasised meeting my desires first and principal.

Avoid performing as Ashley did at the same time as she have become in excessive university. You want to set up smooth boundaries on your relationships if you need them to achieve success over the long run and produce happiness to each additives.

four. Calm down and take inventory of approaches you are currently feeling.

You may discover which you aren't able to prioritize your very own necessities every so often due to the reality you are so preoccupied with looking to satisfy the requirements of others which you are oblivious to the emotions which you are experiencing.

In addition, there are situations in which hurrying around and retaining oneself busy is a way of diverting one's hobby faraway from one's very very own feelings and a more essential problem.

If you need to simply start taking care of yourself and revel in a sense of contentment in life, you need to make the effort to figure out how you're feeling so that you can decide out what it's far which you need inside the first area. If you do no longer try this, you can now not be able to well take care of yourself and additionally you cannot be able to experience content material in existence.

You can learn how to nicely slow down thru following the strategies which is probably referred to in this article.

Working difficult and exerting strive for every body else but oneself is a first-class manner to bring about emotions of exhaustion and resentment. Perform the tough procedure of sorting via your sentiments an amazing way to decide the actions you want to take that permits you to meet your personal necessities.

5. Ask for help

At notable instances, I act as if the word "help" is a dirty four-letter term. And alas, that has been my undoing a protracted manner too regularly in my lifestyles.

Putting yourself first can also furthermore, but, appear to others as despite the fact that you are looking for help.

There have become a time period once I was taking walks on a large assignment for my region of employment. I was resolved to complete this method on my own in order that I would no longer ought to disturb any of my coworkers with my questions or concerns about it.

The reality became that one individual could not in all likelihood entire this employer, and with the useful aid of insisting that I must do all of it by myself, I changed into depriving myself of sleep and spending a awesome deal lots less time with my accomplice for a number of consecutive weeks. At art work, it is going with out announcing that Ashley became a grouchy man or woman.

After suffering to do all the paintings by myself for severa weeks and receiving a stern reprimand from my husband, I determined to subsequently ask my coworkers for assist. As it grew to emerge as out, it modified into no longer a massive issue to them, and after they contributed, the project changed into completed in half of of of the time I had predicted it might take.

It is time to are looking for help even as you aren't able to offer in your personal necessities. It appears that during spite of the whole lot, it's far now not one of these horrible four-letter phrase in spite of the whole lot.

If you spend the bulk of your lifestyles placing distinctive humans's desires earlier than your very very own, there may be a super hazard that you may forget about approximately the way to located your self first. If you take a look at the advice in this newsletter, you may make sure that your necessities are addressed at the same time as moreover developing big relationships with exceptional humans. And in case you located yourself first, you can discover the pleasure and profound sense of achievement which you have been looking for all this time but had been unable to discover till now.

Chapter 3: Take Immediate Action

Grow on your non-public body the seeds of motion a good way to help propel you forward within the pursuit of the desires and goals you have set for yourself.

You Get Started While Everyone Else Puts It Off.

When you have were given arrived at alternatives which are crystal clear, the subsequent diploma is to take right away movement for you to get you one step towards attaining your desires and interests.

It isn't important for the ones moves to be huge or of a in particular most vital type; as a substitute, they must be actions so that you can get subjects rolling and moving in the proper path.

Therefore, however the reality that some people dilly-dally, positioned things off, and hold to take away the belief of their desires till the next day, until the day after that, and the week after that... You take a step as an lousy lot as the plate, firmly greedy your bat with both hands, and also you start to take a swing... Getting to recognize from any disasters you could have, and then trying once more whilst the use of what you have got discovered from your previous attempts... Keep trying all all over again until your failures turn out to be the achievements you've got were given got constantly dreamed of conducting to your life.

Once upon a time, the mythical ice hockey participant Wayne Gretzky said:

If you do no longer even try, you could fail each unmarried time.

You Make Gains Where Others Make Losses

We stay in a society wherein human beings spend coins without lots notion. People are willing to detail with their tough-earned coins to shop for worthless objects within the preference of experiencing a quick enjoy of contentment and pride in the course in their days. Despite this, they pay no attention via the usage of any manner to the prolonged-time period repercussions of their movements and absolve themselves of any duty for their future.

On the possibility hand, you aren't like unique human beings. You limit your spending to the necessities, avoiding frivolous purchases everywhere feasible. Because of this, you're capable of lead a modest way of life, avoid falling into debt, generate long-term monetary riches, and keep your happiness.

You Create While Others Destroy is a Proverb.

The large majority of human beings are liable to falling into the trap of self-sabotage at the identical time as on the same time adverse the livelihoods and objectives of others thru consistent grievance, uncertainty, and mockery. In addition to this, they ponder the query of why their lives do now not beautify thru time.

On the other hand, you aren't a destructor but rather a creator. To create some element new, you ought to first make bigger powerful and empowering behavior that train your thoughts, body, and coronary coronary heart for the journey that lies in advance. You help distinct people in developing their aspirations and bringing them to success in the worldwide spherical them. And via living in concord with the ordinary forces of life, which assist guide you along your course closer to the attainment of your goals and dreams, you assist to nurture the surroundings as properly.

You Carry Out the Desires of Other People

You, but, are taking existence's lemons, turning them into lemonade, and growing a fortune as a forestall cease result, at the same time as others are longing for brighter days and hoping that life will offer them some lemonade.

You set up difficult art work at the identical time as others sit once more and daydream, making development every and every day inside the course of the broader imaginative and prescient a good way to make all your goals come actual.

You Run the Same Danger That Others Fear.

There are clearly an immoderate amount of human beings on this society who are fearful of venturing out of doors the confines of their comfort zones. They are afraid of the options they will be about to make further to the acts they may be about to take due to the truth they worry the unknown, the abnormal, and the uncertainty that comes on the element of those alternatives. They are oblivious to the reality that the inspiration of existence is built on unpredictability. Without the detail of marvel, existence could be silly and uninteresting. You are actually lucky that this isn't a situation that you often enjoy. In element of fact, you do now not shy away from living on the brink and aren't afraid to take calculated dangers, both of which supply you that plenty closer to achieving your most coveted goals and aspirations.

You Continue While Others Give Up

You persevere no matter the truth that others give up even as the going becomes harsh, disturbing, and hard to manage emotionally and physical.

You are conscious that there's no such difficulty as a failure in existence; in fact, you do now not even understand what the word "failure" manner. This phrase satisfactory has any this means that for those individuals who restoration their stare upon the impediments that lie in their path and accomplish that with a sorrowful expression on their face that communicates a enjoy of hopelessness and resignation.

It has been asserted that perseverance, chiefly subjects, is of extra importance than both originality or intelligence or the buildup of life revel in.

Chapter 4: Share Your Modest Victories

We all have dreams that we would really like to carry out, and along the street, we would love to take pride in engaging in even the smallest of these dreams. Our lives gain importance via the pursuit of desires, which furthermore help us in growing into extra admirable versions of ourselves. Have you ever located forth numerous attempts to reap a big intention, virtually to give up in the long run? Have you ever commenced out working inside the path of your purpose, but then discovered out that it's miles absolutely an insurmountable impediment which you cannot conquer?

As human beings, we have a herbal potential to peer issues and to pretty actually chastise ourselves for irrelevant conduct. In our brains, we're short to pick out terrible performances that could deliver emotions of disgrace to the surface. When we revel in what we understand to be failure, our questioning can drag us down, which generally ends in us giving up on our hopes and goals.

What, consequently, is the crucial issue to correctly completing the ones goals. People which can be a success often accomplish notable topics; the query is, how do they do it? The manner you maintain in thoughts the objectives and barriers which have been set in advance than you is the unmarried maximum vital element.

Perspective and frame of thoughts

People have a propensity to feature the accomplishments of others to each right fortune or innate talents that provide them a bonus inside the pursuit in their dreams. Yes, that is some thing that can appear; although, the bulk of the time it's miles due to a particular thoughts-set in addition to a way of considering their dreams of their entirety.

Take for example the American entrepreneur Thomas Edison, who is credited with inventing the lightbulb. Edison made approximately 10,000 attempts to make a lightbulb, that may be a large quantity of "screw ups" earlier than ultimately achieving achievement. In spite of the truth that he had failed numerous times earlier than, he declared, "I even have now not failed. I've truly decided 10,000 one-of-a-kind strategies wherein it won't function.

To placed it another way, he come to be able to transform his failures into achievements as a proper away end give up end result of his attitude, which emerge as centered on succeeding in vicinity of failing. It is fairly obvious that he had a body of mind and an optimistic point of view that enabled him to enjoy the ones tiny accomplishments and see them as achievements.

As I have become announcing earlier, it's far pretty simple for us to criticize and belittle ourselves for insignificant mistakes and setbacks. What approximately all of our insignificant however incredible victories? The irony of the scenario is that whilst we're quick to feel down about our failures, we nearly never make the effort to experience our accomplishments, irrespective of the truth that this is in which the real magic occurs.

Cheer the Little Victories

Realizing that our critical objectives will no longer be executed right away, within the coming week, or maybe in the coming 12 months, but that that is best is the maximum crucial step towards wearing out fulfillment. We will be inclined to pay attention on the very last goals in area of the severa and critical moves that ought to be taken to achieve the ones dreams.

For this purpose, it is vital to recognize and honor one's accomplishments, no matter how modest. The hassle with no longer doing this is that it in the end reasons us to lose our motivation, and our motivation is what keeps us at the right route and offers us the power to hold pushing in advance until we reach the summit of the mountain.

A lack of motivation usually takes place whilst we aren't capable of efficiently study the gap that separates us from the accomplishment of our desires. If we give up now, we are able to in no manner recognize whether or not or not or no longer or no longer the goal is in truth just during the nook, but if we hold to remember that it's far even though to date away, we can live fooled into wondering that it is despite the fact that thus far away.

As a give up stop end result, it is critical which you make it a component to have a great time the final touch of each of your smaller desires along the way. Recognizing our accomplishments, regardless of how minor, turns on the reward circuits in our brains and causes the manufacturing of chemical materials that give us a enjoy of pleasure similarly to a happiness trouble, which in turn motivates us to paintings tougher towards our subsequent purpose.

A essential hassle is appreciation.

In existence, appreciation can be undervalued at times, and as a quit end result, we often fail to apprehend what we've finished and what we had been given. Appreciating the modest accomplishments we attain and the baby steps we take along the way can propose the distinction among fulfillment and failure.

A lack of appreciation and thankfulness might likely positioned us at the precarious path of dropping the capability to understand the importance of our very insignificant achievements. We are acknowledging that we've come an extended manner toward accomplishing our desires at the same time as we've were given amusing insignificant victories. It is a fallacy that we will simplest collect success as quickly as we've got attained that elusive intention; in thing of fact, we are typically making improvement toward our goals.

Establishing Patterns That Lead to Achievement

Successful conduct equal achievement. It is not unusual expertise that forming new behavior and converting modern-day ones can be tough, specifically because of the truth our brains have a hard time adjusting to new workout routines. However, recognizing and praising even the smallest of your accomplishments will let you form the behavior you want and preserve you stimulated to preserve going.

Because our brains need top notch remarks, allowing yourself to be rewarded will bring about the development of an "addiction to development," as a manner to encourage your mind to want to move straight away to the following levels.

Recognize the Significance of Being within the Present Moment

The question now's, what exactly is it that makes a dependancy powerful? The key is to understand the significance of the right here and now and to make it a factor to comprehend and experience even the maximum inconsequential victories along the way. We have a tendency to dismiss the proper here and now as it seems to be unimportant, and we mistakenly enjoy that the movements we perform in the now won't have any impact on who we're inside the destiny.

You need to recognize that you best have the triumphing moment and make the most of it via making an investment within the insignificant info over the path of a prolonged time period. The accumulation of small successes over an extended term is what ends in large accomplishments.

Take, for example, the situation in which you want to build up statistics on a whole new subject matter. Reading ten pages of a e-book on a modern-day difficulty remember these days will now not substantially growth your information, and likely no longer even reading ten pages day after today and ten pages the day after if you need to extensively boom your facts. However, it is the cumulative impact of all of those small steps, like analyzing 10 pages constant with day, a good way to ultimately can help you collect a whole information of the contemporary mission depend.

To located it some exclusive way, whilst reading those 10 pages an afternoon might not seem like a huge deal within the warmth of the on the spot, it's miles an crucial step in the gadget of wearing out your goal and mastering the potential to pay attention.

How to Rejoice in Your Many Successes

Keeping all of this in mind, it's miles vital that the accomplishments that we chalk as an lousy lot as "little wins" be recognized and valued for what they sincerely are. When it entails identifying whether or now not or no longer or not we are a fulfillment, motivation performs a large function, and the capability to apprehend and apprehend even the smallest victories is critical. Here is the way to capitalize on the importance of very minor accomplishments.

1. Chunk down large goals into greater viable ones.

Even if it can be tempting to do so, you need to keep away from concentrating on the wider photo. Make positive that you set reasonable and feasible goals for yourself as a way to allow you to peer your development extra certainly. These mini victories will assist you experience better approximately each and every one in each of your little one steps.

When we are confronted with a difficult cause, our thoughts have a propensity to fall into the sample of setting subjects off till later. This trouble may be avoided through way of putting greater possible goals.

2. Give your self a praise.

Consider what it's miles that brings you the maximum satisfaction, and try this on every occasion you end one of the steps. This could be performing some component as smooth as trying to find yourself a cup of your preferred coffee or as concerned as happening an actual holiday. The brain is knowledgeable to become more stimulated on the equal time because it has some issue to assume and expect.

three. Don't Pressure Yourself

Even while there are minor accomplishments along the manner, you run the threat of feeling like a failure in case you set your desires with hard dates and anticipate to benefit them. Make a while barriers as bendy as viable, and you will locate that this boosts each your happiness and your motivation as you have fun the accomplishment of even the smallest of dreams.

four. Keep Tabs on Your Advancement

You might also remind yourself of processes a ways you have were given come in the direction of undertaking your cause via writing down or recording your development along the way. Sometimes we are tempted to surrender due to the fact we're blind to how near we're to undertaking our goals or have forgotten how a good buy art work we've were given already established. Noting down all of the victories, no matter how insignificant they may seem, may be a prize in and of itself.

five. Alter the manner you test matters.

It is feasible that the eventual objective will appear insurmountable if we area too much emphasis on it. You can also want to discover it useful to imagine that as opposed to trekking a super mountain, you're descending a mountain that has a few splendid consuming places (rewards) alongside the manner that you can prevent at and loosen up along the manner. Taking pleasure within the little victories along the way will make the fulfillment of your prolonged-term targets appear plenty much less daunting in the end.

The Crux of the Matter

If you want to keep your motivation on the equal time as walking closer to your dreams, one of the most vital subjects you can do is learn how to have fun even the little victories. Find a way to have amusing each time you reach a modern day benchmark, whether or not or now not or not it is by means of placing a movie big name at the corresponding day of your calendar, indulging in an extravagant lunch for one, or spending time with a close to pal. When you have positioned in the attempt to acquire a purpose, you in fact deserve a praise of some kind.

The picks that we make are impacted thru our thoughts. These choices pave the way to fulfillment. This is a traditional example of a prophecy that comes actual at some point of itself. Fortuitously, a high-quality range of leaders have hassle celebrating their victories. Many refuse to move due to the truth they take into account it to be a accident. Some may additionally experience irritated even after a extraordinary win. Because of this, their performance, the manner they manipulate their personnel, or maybe their monetary consequences are all right away impacted.

For this motive, appreciating your successes is a really important exercise. No rely in which you are in lifestyles, whether or now not or now not you simply landed your first purchaser in your commercial corporation or had been given the assignment of your dreams, you ought to revel in each and each success along the manner. There are not any random occurrences. There is a purpose in the returned of the whole thing that takes place. It is always feasible to duplicate achievement. Make first rate which you take note of every one, that you talk them with the correct human beings, which you give a boost to the concept that you are transferring in the right path, and which you are a person who has brilliant fortune on their issue all the time.

The first-rate victories are regularly the modest ones. This consists of getting super encounters at a networking event, discovering your information, and touchdown your first customers, in addition to having a exceptional revel in with the human beings you care approximately most in the worldwide... Celebrating one's accomplishments is important to feeling carried out. So maintain celebrating.

"Those who're a achievement are capable of maintain momentum. The more they gain their desires, the more they choice to gain even extra desires, and the more they make bigger techniques to advantage those goals. Likewise, whilst someone is suffering, they have got a extra propensity to fall farther and similarly inside the once more of, that might even end up a self-perfect prophecy.

Chapter 5: Journalize Your Activities And Achievements

At your vicinity of employment, its miles important to establish and show your desires, as doing so permits you to bolster inside your career on the equal time as simultaneously mastering essential competencies. Keeping a piece pocket e book which you document your assignments in and your successes in on a ordinary basis is a excellent method to show your development and hold your self prompted. This article will offer an cause of what a piece mag is, the benefits of retaining a chunk diary, further to the moves you want to do so one can assemble your very very private art work mag.

What exactly is a "paintings mag" regardless of the truth that?

A record that allows you hold tune of your development at art work is known as a "art work magazine." A artwork pocket book is a useful tool for preserving track of responsibilities, goals, mind, and different reminders. Keeping a bit mag may be done in lots of methods, which includes by handwriting entries in a pocket book or with the aid of typing notes on a computer. Both the layout and the content material of a bit diary are decided through using the person who is keeping the mag and thru way of what works fine for them.

The blessings of maintaining a piece magazine

Keeping a magazine at art work may be beneficial in a number of strategies, at the side of the subsequent:

Capability of monitoring one's private ordinary performance.

You can music your development over a term and note how some distance you have got come thru maintaining a mag of your routines and sports at art work. When it's time for usual performance critiques or at the equal time as you're looking for a brand new characteristic, this could be of specific help to you. You can skip decrease returned on your paintings mag at any time to have a observe a list of your maximum ultra-contemporary achievements or the abilties which you have honed whilst working on particular initiatives.

Discover areas in which you could make improvements.

You can be able to apprehend no longer certainly your achievements in the place of job however additionally opportunities for private development in case you keep a piece magazine. For instance, you may find that the instances on that you start artwork in advance are the times on that you have the pleasant fulfillment in phrases of productiveness. Then, you may introduce new behaviors to help you in getting started out out in advance within the day, which includes setting out the time desk for tomorrow the night earlier than. A art work log also can show you whether or now not you are making any habitual mistakes, which can be useful in identifying which of them want to be addressed first.

Take notes on your actual thoughts.

There are instances if you have an concept related to your business enterprise, but you honestly do not have the time to research it right now. Instead of letting that brilliant new innovative belief slip away, jot it down for your work diary. Because of this, you'll be able to return to all of your modern thoughts at a later time, at the same time as you may have more time to bear in mind them.

A guide to preserving and the usage of a work mag

Try following the steps stated beneath to get your place of job journaling business enterprise off to a high-quality start:

1. Pick a layout for your magazine.

Determine in that you would love to maintain your notes and write them down. The use of a separate pocket ebook, a document stored to your computer, or software program handy on-line are all commonplace options for maintaining a mag. This preference is solely determined via one's very personal options, for the reason that each of those alternatives have deserves. Try using a notepad, as an instance, in case you feel that writing topics down with the resource of hand brings you a experience of delight. Try using an app that helps you to take notes on-line if you'd as an alternative convey your notes round with you anywhere you move. Pick some component that now not most effective makes it clean as a manner to put in writing notes on every occasion you enjoy the need to, however moreover allows smooth retrieval of those notes whilst it is time to head over them.

2. Determine the goals of your artwork.

Make a list of some of the professional accomplishments you purpose to collect. Your dreams can be reflective of your not unusual plans for your career or the subjects which you are focusing on at your present day place of job. As an example, the goals of a social media supervisor can encompass being promoted to the region of advertising and advertising director in the next years or growing the social following of a client via thirty percentage. When you are defining your goals, attempt to be as clean as you likely can, and deliver your self a final date just so the cause can be a good deal much less complicated to gain.

three. Make a way for the way you'll collect those desires.

Record in writing how you propose to transport toward reaching your objectives on the start of every new week. Because doing so locations you in a greater proactive thoughts-set for the rest of the week, the excellent time to hold this out is first difficulty on a Monday morning. Additionally, it offers you with certain sports to perform ultimately of the week so you are in no way at a loss for what to perform.

4. Keep a document of your achievements and regions for improvement.

Keep a report of a few aspect you deem large and maintain it with you at some point of the week. This carries gadgets you finish, belongings you don't get a hazard to complete, errors you're making, ideas, and notes from meetings. You will become more acquainted with the use of your paintings journal, at which element you may realize which components of your workday to report and which of them to bypass. Record as heaps as you could as you get began, even though. Record the entirety.

five. Be positive to often observe your accomplishments, behavior, and destiny plans.

Find some time on the prevent of every week to study over again thru your paintings log and study the dreams you've got set further to the quantity of progress you've got made within the course of reaching those goals. Make use of this facts the following week even as you put your new desires for the following week.

In addition to this, it's far a smart circulate to every now and then look at through everything of your mag. Begin at the beginning of your journal and undergo it, seeking out styles which you could not have recognized. It's viable, for instance, which you find out Fridays to be the least productive day of the week, or that you time table an excessive sort of meetings on Tuesdays. These opinions furthermore offer you a clearer photograph of your longer-time period dreams and the stairs you have taken to get inside the route of attaining them.

Keeping a piece mag: a few beneficial suggestions

If you need to get the most from your paintings magazine, attempt implementing the subsequent pointers:

Talk about it with different humans.

You might want to bear in mind letting different people see your work magazine, at the least in component. If you permit someone else check via your paintings mag, they is probably conscious tremendous forms of conduct that you have neglected. You can also furthermore communicate it with a supervisor simply so they may be aware about the private dreams you have got set for your self. Sharing your art work mag together together with your supervisor is a incredible technique to document your request for assist from a superior within the event which you want a few element from them that will help you obtain your purpose, whether or now not or no longer that purpose is related to your undertaking or your career.

Make a duplicate for your self.

It is pretty recommended which you preserve a backup or reproduction of your paintings diary constantly. One of the benefits of preserving a bit mag on your laptop or on line is the fact that it is straightforward to make copies of entries in the magazine. Consider typing up your notes or photocopying the pages at regular periods if you however decide upon writing topics down. If you prefer to write matters down, however, maintain to attain this.

Use colors

When it involves organizing your art work pocket book, using colorings is a first-rate way to transport. As an example, you may write or highlight all your achievements in green. After that, at the same time as it's time to mirror at the achievements you performed eventually of that yr, you'll be able to discover them correctly to your magazine. Create your very private color-coding machine to help you without problems put together and become privy to the subjects which may be crucial to you.

Create your writing on the same time every day.

If you need to growth a everyday, you ought to attempt to write to your paintings mag at the identical time each day or every week. This will assist you set up a recurring. Before you leave the place of job or flip off your pc at the quit of each day, you may discover it beneficial to write down down in your work mag. The benefits of preserving a work mag are maximized whilst the pocket e-book is used regularly, and developing a writing ordinary will increase the probability that you may use the magazine extra frequently.

Positive reinforcement is the important component to experiencing emotions of success. One effective technique for generating these forms of satisfactory rewards is to preserve a magazine log of 1's activities in addition to one's achievements. You might also need to have the opportunity to mirror on the sports activities, achievements, and lifestyles instructions that took place in some unspecified time in the future of the day in case you maintain a mag. Not quality in your very own growth as an person, however additionally for plenty distinct elements of your lifestyles, journaling can be a without a doubt beneficial device.

Chapter 6: Treat Failure As An Experiment

Both fulfillment and failure are inevitable components of our life. But acknowledging your shortcomings and growing above them is a hard mission to accomplish. Failures are truly a constructing block on the street to fulfillment given that they regularly illuminate the notable way to keep. Failures of every type need to be treated in the best way possible. However, which will put together yourself for success, you need to discover ways to confront your fears and disappointments while lifestyles knock you down. Are you unsure approximately your capability to do the project?

The following is a listing of the fine techniques which could help you in disregarding past setbacks and getting lower again to your ordinary conduct without issues:

1. An Environment That Is Emotionally Motivating

It is normal to have an emotional harm at the same time as you fail at something, particularly if the failure turned into your fault. Nearly 1/2 of of of respondents (forty eight%) widely known that pressure has a terrible have an impact on on every their artwork and personal lives. Because of this, it's miles surely critical to pull yourself far from the emotional usa and supply yourself time to get higher. Nobody anticipates that you'll get better any time quick.

Take some time and look for an emotionally motivating putting for you to offer you with the power to conquer the setbacks you have were given skilled. During this degree, you are obligated to direct your interest within the direction of any first rate additives of your environment that you could understand. Your stress levels can flow down and the healing device can glide alongside more brief in case you are in an environment that is emotionally healing.

2. Make a plan to your upcoming sports activities activities.

Moving earlier is the satisfactory approach for mitigating the destructive outcomes of past setbacks. Make a preference approximately what steps you could take next. Your next moves ought to be powerful to the issue wherein they supply you the effects you have got been searching out. If the effects of your failure can not be undone, you have to search for opportunity routes that could lead to success. There is still time for you to plan your moves and your method for handling the contemporary state of affairs, even though you haven't made preparations for the possibility that you could experience failure in the future. It will offer you with a distraction in your mind and assist you in working over the setbacks that you have skilled.

"Losers give up after they enjoy failure. Winners are people who fail on their way to achievement." — Robert Kiyosaki

3. Learn from your mistakes with the useful resource of turning them into training opportunities

Your successes may be constructed on the muse of your failures. Every setback you go through locations you one step inside the course of triumph, and in the end, it famous to you the direction that you want to conform with to acquire your dreams. It is critical to advantage awareness from the errors you have got got dedicated within the past and to make sure that they may be by no means repeated.

And the possibility exists as a way to investigate that thru your errors. The errors you made that introduced approximately your failure provide perception into the manner which you want to be completing the interest. And we virtually need to have this with the intention to acquire fulfillment in existence. You will no longer require the course of anybody else going forward due to the fact your preceding mistakes are pointing you in the proper direction.

four. Errors are Unavoidable; There Is No Need to Mourn Over Them

We all make errors. The majority of state-of-the-art a hit businesspeople had their start as unsuccessful marketers, however they in the end have grow to be subjects round and executed top notch fulfillment. There is simply no disgrace in committing errors or failing at some thing. If one does now not make an effort to well teach oneself on the way to do jobs, it's far inevitable that they may fail numerous times.

As a result, it's miles essential to hold in thoughts that you may pull your self up from the muck of your past mistakes and set your attractions on the route in advance. In spite of the truth that you apprehend what it is need to fail, you need to now not be afraid to strive yet again. Failure is a necessary step on the road to achievement; by the use of gaining an facts of the proper technique to perform operations, you could boom the danger of reaching success that is sustainable through the years.

five. Look for Sources of Motivation

In cutting-edge-day international, there can be an abundance of humans that specialize inside the art work of motivating personnel to carry out to the first-rate in their skills. Look to them for mind and motivation. Because of the internet, it's miles now less difficult than ever to speak with folks who live in any part of the area and has grow to be possible to carry the whole global onto a unmarried platform.

Find a deliver of motivation that has the most resonance along with your beyond setbacks and your present times. Try to get them in your detail. You also can find out idea and motivation inside the oldsters which are closest to you, collectively with buddies and circle of relatives. During the hard durations to your life, all you actually need is a person to lean on and cry with because of the reality they might inspire you to push thru and attention at the high first-rate matters of your existence.

6. Reconsider your alternatives and make a undertaking plan for the future

Where did we move incorrect? The reaction to this question will let you in doing an analysis of your actions and identifying whether or not or not or now not or not they have been accountable for your loss of fulfillment. For example, a startup proprietor who's inside the machine of organising their enjoy-hailing corporation is capable of evaluate their actions and determine what triggered the sudden failure of their marketing strategy.

It's feasible that they've been no longer capable of offer effective offerings, that the software emerge as beside the aspect for them, or any sort of different factors contributed to their failure. In a similar manner, you may figure out the errors that passed off or that you made that have been the number one humans to your failure. This lets in you to apprehend the behaviors that cause failure and plan out your next steps on this shape of manner which you in no way allow the ones behaviors to rise up yet again.

"If you fail at some element truly as quickly as, it does no longer endorse that you could fail at everything else you strive." - Marilyn Monroe

7. Anticipate the Best Possible Outcomes

You have to now not decrease your expectations, even after experiencing a string of setbacks. The trauma that is because of the fear of failing can regularly save you someone from getting over the screw ups that they have got professional however their extraordinary efforts. However, now could be the time as a way to picture yourself succeeding, and you need to accomplish that. You need to not be frightened of failing; as an opportunity, you want to plot to prevail by means of way of remembering the things you've got were given decided through your preceding errors.

You can help yourself preserve your hopes up and your spirits alive with the resource of watching for a tangible result in your work. Create a intellectual photograph of your self becoming a fulfillment, after which make a plan outlining the steps you accept as true with gets you there. The high-quality technique for overcoming your setbacks is to double down on your efforts and confront the problem head on.

Do no longer allow setbacks damage your conceitedness. Maintain a immoderate fashionable of morality, and fight the urge to doubt your self. You can acquire success and preserve failure at bay in case you train yourself on a manner to succeed in tough times and use what you have got a have a look at. You can accumulate the top of success if you have a supportive environment, strong motivators, and the capability to draw facts out of your past mistakes.

Our minds have not in fact superior all that an lousy lot. Despite this, we ought to determine out the way to get round in this contemporary environment with our historic brains. It makes excellent revel in, going decrease again to the time of the cavemen, at the same time as ignoring a danger or an hassle may also were deadly to our species. Our minds are antiquated, and as a end result, they'll be stressed out to cognizance greater on the bad than at the remarkable. It is consequently understandable why our minds aren't nicely-organized to address setbacks.

But the reality is that errors can be quite treasured. Now that you've experimented with some thing and acquired remarks, you can take movement based on the statistics you gathered. This is what Bob Ross had to mention about it: "We don't make mistakes. It's all in truth a sequence of lucky coincidences." With every new attempt, you flow into that loads inside the course of accomplishing your intention! Therefore, fail fast, fail ahead, and have an wonderful snigger about it with the humans you care approximately.

Therefore, think of each unsuccessful strive as an experiment. When you do some thing again and again, you may glaringly get higher at it. The extra you install strive, the extra information you're taking in, and the better off you may be. There aren't any such things as actual failures. There isn't a single mistake. Every time you attempt a few trouble and it might no longer training consultation, take it as an possibility to attempt some issue else and get better at it.

Chapter 7: Self-Complementing And Receiving Them

Complimenting others at art work is crucial for developing and preserving relationships, whether you are a supervisor or a man or woman contributor. Both giving and receiving compliments play a crucial element in this technique. When delivered well, a complement is one of the only strategies to deliver to a few different character how an entire lot fee and appreciation we region on them. Nevertheless, those reputedly right encounters may be wonder hard to govern for each the man or woman doing the giving and the individual doing the receiving. In a number of my earliest studies, which come to be later posted below the title "What to Do When Praise Makes You Uncomfortable," I positioned that in spite of the reality that the most common response to being recognized is a feel of being valued (noted thru way of 88% of respondents), nearly 70% of respondents related the act of each giving and receiving praise with emotions of embarrassment or pain.

My research has demonstrated that the process of giving and receiving compliments often brings up a notable deal of hysteria for all activities worried, however the reality that receiving and giving compliments need to be great opinions and that that is the case the bulk of the time. People who supply compliments frequently fear that they will be perceived as kissing up to the recipient, that their commentary is probably misunderstood, or that it will reason others to feel jealous. People who're on the receiving give up of some thing bad often enjoy as despite the truth that they do no longer deserve it, strong doubt on the reasons of the person who gave it to them, or worry that they'll now not be able to advantage the equal bring about the destiny.

It has come to my interest that there are strategies for each giving and receiving compliments that assist ruin down some of those obstacles, so making the stumble upon greater satisfactory and conducive to the improvement of accept as true with. It may additionally additionally furthermore seem counterintuitive, but on the way to come to be better at giving compliments, we want to first end up higher at accepting them. Only then are we able to want to enhance our capability to compliment others.

How to Take Pleasure in Being Flattered

Your supervisor or a coworker manages to trap you off guard with a praise, and what have to be a second of pride rather leaves your thoughts spinning as you clumsily navigate a way to respond to them. It's possible that our responses to praises are complicated, but the manner we act in reaction is not. The large majority of human beings are unaware that compliments are normally greater approximately the best who's giving them than about the person that is receiving them. When a person offers you a praise, they're without a doubt revealing how some thing you probably did touched them in some way. It isn't always vital whether or now not or not you compromise or disagree with what they may be pronouncing; what is vital is that you relate to what they will be saying as a present and acquire it. If a chairman or a coworker has been kind to you, the splendid way to answer is to surely say "Thank you." Additionally, if the praise did make a distinction to your lifestyles, you need to allow the person realise. If you be conscious which you are deflecting the praise given to you via every other person through passing the credit rating to a person else, making a funny tale, or clumsily explaining why you do now not deserve it, you can get higher the situation thru using which consist of, "I am strolling on getting better at accepting a reward. Thank you."

The following is a list of possible responses to a reward:

"You're truly welcome, and understanding that brightens my day."

"I really did deliver this masses of concept, and I respect you pointing it out to me."

"Thank you plenty, I in reality fee the truth that you took the time to convey that," you said.

"You're welcome, and it makes me pleased to understand that is how you experience!"

If the other character enhances you at the artwork of every exclusive individual, you need to direct their praise to the ideal individual, as follows:

"I am thrilled to look at that that is the way you enjoy! In aspect of truth, Amanda is the mastermind inside the lower again of this challenge. If you have got were given a 2d, it might truly brighten her day to listen how you enjoy about the situation.

"I ought to want not a few aspect greater than to claim credit score rating for this, however John is the nice who need to get it. When I see him in recent times, I will make certain to relay your feedback to him.

If you get maintain of praise for some aspect that become the result of the blended efforts of a set, make sure to bypass alongside the acknowledgment. Be aware, if you are the chief of the institution, that the individual can be complimenting you at the placement that you play in guiding your humans; consequently, it's miles critical that to procure the praise first, and then famend the artwork of your team:

"I would really like to thank you for noticing; it's far very encouraging to listen that. Over the direction of the beyond few weeks, each member of our group has been putting in some of tough paintings in this mission. I will speak your input with every person at our upcoming meeting.

It is essential to keep in mind that our ingrained responses to compliments have been shaped over the direction of our existence, and much like a few exclusive dependancy, changing the ones responses could require aware effort and consistent exercise. During the following week, pay attention to the manner you and others react to compliments, and strive using a number of the responses which have been furnished above on your very own interactions. After a couple of weeks, you may comprehend that it is not all that difficult to simply respond with "Thank you!"

Complimenting Someone in a Way That Really Means Something

A critical thing of powerful leadership is the capacity to provide compliments and famend the accomplishments of others. On the alternative hand, only some human beings are familiar with the way to efficaciously deliver it out. I honestly have spoken with and perplexed hundreds of human beings over the path of the past ten years a terrific manner to advantage an know-how of what constitutes an powerful supplement. My research has shown that the messages which can be maximum likely to be remembered and to have an impact are those which might be authentic, specific, and center at the manufacturing approach. A strong reward may match an prolonged way, so here are a few tips at the way to supply one.

Be proper to yourself. The sincerity of your purpose is the issue of any supplement that sticks out as being the maximum important. Do now not compliment the man or woman at the way to butter them up in advance than developing a request, melt the blow earlier than giving difficult remarks, or try and cheer them up after creating a mistake. These are all beside the point motives to present a reward. If your aim isn't always real, then your praise will no longer be real each. When human beings see you to be inauthentic in a single place, on the side of your recognition, they may additionally be given as authentic with which you are inauthentic in one of a kind areas. Do no longer compliment someone surely because of the reality you take transport of as real with which you want to; rather, reward someone because you revel in compelled to allow them to understand how their actions effect you or others. This is a incredible rule to examine. Be precise. When you reward someone, you must share your mind in a way that doesn't leave them with any unanswered questions. This is real whether or not or no longer or now not you're supplying remarks or giving instructions. Take, as an example, the phrase "That become super!" (What modified into so tremendous?

"You have my utmost apprehend." (What's the factor?)

"I admire you taking notes at some point of the assembly. Thank you very lots." (Since it's my paintings, I do now not apprehend why you're spotting me.)

When we communicate with distinctive humans, it's miles vital to offer examples and specifics to help the other person apprehend the context of what we're announcing. When we offer a person a reward in a way that is apparent, that character comprehends precisely what we're expressing and why we are announcing it.

Unspecific praise: "Thank you lots for taking notes at some stage in the meeting; you're super!"

Specifically, I complimented John with the aid of way of saying, "John, I am aware that it's far your duty to take notes in the course of the assembly; despite the fact that, due to the fact you do it so effectively, I am superb that I can lighten up and awareness on acting my assignment." Thank you."

Put your hobby no longer clearly on the prevent surrender end result however moreover at the technique. According to the findings of my studies, humans's number one desire isn't to be stated for the give up product itself, but alternatively for the tool and artwork that went into making that give up product. Compliments which may be often centered at the quit quit result have a tendency to purpose the recipient to fear that they will no longer be capable of accumulate the same bring about the future, which may be bad to the relationship. When you supply someone reputation, you need to display which you appreciate the effort, willpower, ingenuity, or hobby that went into the work that they have got completed.

"Phil, I am astounded via the event you placed up for the purchaser. You have my utmost apprehend." What I can't even start to fathom is the quantity of time, try, and originality that went into making that event a achievement. Thank you very lots for the whole thing you probable did to make this task a fulfillment backstage.

Discuss the repercussions. Keep in thoughts that a reward is commonly more approximately the best who's giving it than the person who is receiving it. When we commend a person, what we're simply doing is letting them comprehend how their moves had an impact on us. Give the person you're complimenting a window into what you professional and the way it impacted you or others, and you will deliver them a powerful complement on the way to live with them. Think about telling humans how their control impacts the organization, how their paintings impacts the results of the organization, and the way their mind-set influences the climate of the organization.

"Jane, I desired to take a second to unique my gratitude for the manner in that you manual our personnel. On my previous organization, I end up continuously afraid to voice my critiques for worry that my supervisor might criticize them. Since the very first day, I positioned the manner you advocated every one folks to talk out and specific our thoughts, and as a end result, I felt safe sufficient to try new things. I actually have some of a laugh on the same time as working for you, and I typically have the effect that I'm improving. Thank you."

The Checklist for Receiving Compliments

When you are subsequent in a characteristic in that you revel in compelled to provide someone a praise, take a second earlier than you accomplish that and answer the questions which may be listed beneath.

Authentic: What about this person makes me suppose I've seen them earlier than?

Specifically, what become it that I encountered or found?

What steps did they must go through in order to benefit their goals?

What form of an effect did their movements have at the crew and on me?

As you gain experience and grow to be more professional at the art of giving and accepting meaningful compliments, the solutions to the ones questions will in the long run grow to be as herbal to you as respiratory. You are loose to get started out to your exercising right away. Who became it that you had bear in mind to praise all alongside?

People in control positions will be predisposed to be their non-public worst critics. Complimenting oneself isn't always frequently a task that comes with out issues. Compliments, however, are the great approach of improving our experience of self confidence and preserving the superb reinforcement. In addition to that, it's far an high-quality technique to keep your motivation up.

The query now could be: how are we able to praise ourselves with out discovering as immodest? Try to be your private largest supporter. Compliments can are to be had each spoken or written shape, depending on the giver's preference. But thinking about that it's miles a letter to your very very own self, in reality located it in writing! Give yourself a constant flow into of compliments. Every time you "fail," whenever you get better, and each time you win, regardless of how modest the victory can be. You are first rate, and due to that, you are properly to your manner to conducting the whole thing your coronary heart dreams and you are more than insanely deserving of it.

Chapter 8: Charm Your Way Towards Success

Develop the seeds of charisma and enchantment within your very very personal man or woman, thinking about this can help propel you earlier on the direction to undertaking your dreams and aims.

You are the Leader, and others follow in your footsteps.

As we skip in advance in lifestyles, it is crucial to surround ourselves with feature models who can guide us inside the course of success. On the possibility hand, a number of humans get this piece of recommendation stressed with a leash. And when topics pass notably, as they frequently will (it's far the truth of existence), the ones human beings take no responsibility and blame their mentors for main them down the wrong path instead of taking duty for their very private actions.

On the opportunity hand, you aren't someone who follows others. Yes, you be aware of the advice of others; however, you aren't tethered to a leash, and you've got a comprehensive know-how that you should make your non-public alternatives and create your very non-public future based totally on what is outstanding for you in every state of affairs and scenario. This is the case irrespective of the fact that you do take the recommendation of others.

You employ this experience to draw fanatics who will help you alongside your adventure toward the fulfillment of your desires by way of manner of providing you with help along the manner. And as extra human beings start to study in your footsteps, you may in turn be able to help the ones people in the focus in their dreams thru imparting them with private route, idea, and have an impact on.

You Give Praise While Others Give Criticism

People are very prepared to condemn and issue the finger at others for the acts, alternatives, or behavior that they themselves have delivered on. This might not do some thing but convey down people's spirits, and it's miles not exactly the best technique for making friends and gaining effect with others.

On the other hand, you have got a profound attention that the relationships you cultivate are the the usage of stress at the back of your lifestyles's prolonged-time period and ongoing fulfillment. If you do not have the backing of a sturdy community of different individuals who are supporting you along side your motive, you're doomed to end up a sad failure. In moderate of this, you venture to inspire and encourage others thru praising the art work that they have got finished, thereby boosting their spirits, arrogance, and experience of cause in a way that permits you to bring about a relationship this is collectively beneficial, thereby allowing all events worried to benefit extra of what it's far in existence that they cost the maximum.

You Give, While Others Take From You

The idea of getting what you want whilst you need it's miles the foundation upon which the cultural sample of everyday immediately gratification is built. People have the thoughts-set that within the event that they take, take, and take a few more, they'll sooner or later benefit what it's miles in lifestyles that they choice. Because they will be so preoccupied with themselves, they'll be oblivious to the reality that so that you can accumulate what they preference in the long run, they'll want to sacrifice what they have got inside the brief run.

You, alternatively, have an entire comprehension of the reality which you need to provide to one-of-a-kind human beings what it is which you would really like to get keep of. This concept makes me do not forget the vacuum principle, which states that a void is created every time you deliver your strength out into the universe. This void can be perception of as an empty place. In order to reestablish the precarious equilibrium of existence, this void wants to be full of the identical form of power that became earlier than gift.

When you've got were given were given this understanding, you are able to supply to people with none expectations, whether or not or not or not it's gives, your power, top notch feelings, or a while. Because of this power, over the years you'll be capable of enchantment your manner into the lives of many human beings, in order to frequently bring your aspirations into fact inside the most unexpected way.

You Love Even Though Others Hate You

There are moments even as it appears as even though our international is entire to the brim with lots hatred that, in personal, it feels as no matter the reality that every body secretly despises each person else for reasons which may be often very minor and unimportant.

You, alternatively, stay on because of the fact on your love. You have a deep appreciation for the planet, one-of-a-type human beings, your art work, your frame, and your lifestyles.

You are able to see opportunities in which others handiest see troubles; you're able to domesticate sturdy bonds and relationships in case you want to final an entire life on the same time as others ruin theirs. This is because the feeling of love focuses your hobby at the high notable components of lifestyles.

You take notes because the others talk.

Everyone has a tale to inform, a highbrow want to experience desired, and the selection to discover a person who will listen to their issues. Everyone is looking for a person to pay attention to their memories. These people are so preoccupied with their non-public needs and issues that they may be completely oblivious to the requirements of others.

To enhance in existence, we want to emerge as adept at finding solutions to the annoying situations confronted with the aid of others. Listening, wondering, after which performing in a manner a exquisite manner to bring about the solutions that we need to hold into our personal lives are the steps that need to be taken to perform this intention. In thing of truth, is it simply that an prolonged manner-fetched to assume that the those who pay hobby extra than they communicate are folks who're the most remarkable and who have the excellent experience of approach?

You are very lots part of this organization of human beings. You hold your ears open for hints, possibilities, and answers that present themselves, with the intention to assist you in making particular headway within the route of the achievement of your desires and goals.

You Laugh in the Face of Others' Sadness.

While maximum humans choose to scowl whilst confronted with demanding conditions or problems, you're able to hold a grin for your face no matter this. A clean grin can speedy modify your angle, compel you to test the lighter aspect of lifestyles, open the doorways to new possibilities, and ship robust lifestyles-transforming strength toward individuals inside your area of have an effect on.

Chapter 9: Mindset Shifts Embracing Growth

In the hollow financial disaster of "Simple Ways to Change Your Life in 2024," we embark on a transformative journey, delving into the profound realm of thoughts-set shifts. At the helm of this exploration is the empowering idea of the Growth Mindset.

1.1 Embrace a Growth Mindset:

As we stand on the precipice of exchange, it's miles crucial to widely known the profound affect our thoughts-set wields over the trajectory of our lives. Coined thru the use of psychologist Carol Dweck, the Growth Mindset serves as a radiant beacon, illuminating the path within the course of self-discovery and improvement.

Unlocking the Power of Belief in Personal Growth:

The Growth Mindset transcends mere nomenclature; it's miles a philosophy propelling us ahead. Rooted in the records that our capabilities are not fixed but may be cultivated via dedication and try, it holds the transformative energy of believing in the malleability of intelligence and capabilities over time.

Consider this paradigm shift: demanding situations stop to be insurmountable limitations but, as an opportunity, possibilities for analyzing. Embracing a Growth Mindset liberates our capability, turning setbacks into stepping stones closer to profound private growth. By rewriting the narrative of our abilities, we chart a route for limitless opportunities.

Guiding Tips for Fostering a Growth Mindset:

Embrace Challenges: Rather than shying far from disturbing conditions, welcome them as chances to make bigger your abilties and knowledge boom.

Celebrate Effort, Not Just Results: Shift attention from results to the invested attempt. Acknowledge and have amusing the journey of studying.

Learn from Criticism: Instead of viewing criticism as a personal assault, see it as wonderful feedback. Extract valuable insights and use them to refine your approach.

Cultivate Curiosity: Approach the place with a curious thoughts. Ask questions, attempting to find knowledge, and nurture a hunger for continuous getting to know.

Surround Yourself with Growth-Oriented Individuals: Engage with folks who inspire and encourage non-public improvement. Their mind-set can have an effect on and raise your own.

By integrating those practices into your every day existence, you lay the inspiration for a attitude thriving on disturbing situations, viewing effort because the path to mastery, and embracing reading as a perpetual adventure.

As those initial pages unfold, understand the efficiency of a Growth Mindset in guidance your existence towards non-stop development. The adventure has without a doubt commenced, and with every thoughts-set shift, you propel yourself within the direction of the transformative 12 months that awaits.

1.2 Practice Gratitude Daily

Continuing our exploration of mind-set shifts in "Simple Ways to Change Your Life in 2024," our awareness turns to a practice wielding profound transformative energy – every day gratitude.

Explore the Benefits of Gratitude:

Gratitude isn't a fleeting emotion; it's miles a transformative manner of lifestyles reshaping perspectives and raising well-being. In this section, we're going to delve into the benefits of gratitude and provide practical, easy tactics to weave this powerful workout into the cloth of your every day existence.

Transformative Benefits of Gratitude:

Gratitude transcends cultural barriers, tapping into the middle of our humanity. It's more than a polite acknowledgment; it's far a profound popularity of life's first-class components. Consider a few transformative blessings:

Enhanced Mental Well-being: Regular expressions of gratitude are related to lower strain and depression tiers, fostering a powerful intellectual outlook.

Improved Physical Health: Grateful humans frequently report higher physical health, together with improved sleep exceptional and a bolstered immune tool.

Enhanced Relationships: Gratitude deepens connections, fostering a sense of belonging and strengthening interpersonal bonds.

Increased Resilience: Grateful human beings navigate stressful conditions with extra resilience, finding silver linings in hard conditions.

Heightened Self-Esteem: Appreciating the extraordinary factors of lifestyles contributes to a complicated feel of self esteem.

Simple Gratitude Practices for Daily Life:

Gratitude Journal: Dedicate a couple of minutes each day to install writing 3 property you are grateful for. Reflect on the information, savoring the associated feelings.

Morning Gratitude Ritual: Begin your day thru acknowledging three assets you're thankful for, placing a pleasing tone for the day.

Gratitude Jar: Create a gratitude jar, dropping in notes expressing moments of gratitude. Periodically examine those notes for a satisfying reminder of life's benefits.

Express Gratitude to Others: Take time to unique gratitude to friends, family, and co-employees. A heartfelt "thanks" can create a ripple effect of positivity.

Mindful Gratitude Walks: During your every day walks, be aware of the splendor round you. Express gratitude for the sights, sounds, and sensations of the prevailing second.

By incorporating the ones easy gratitude practices into your each day recurring, you embark on a adventure of cultivating a grateful coronary coronary coronary heart. As you encompass the transformative energy of gratitude, may additionally your days be complete of appreciation for the richness of existence.

1.Three Letting Go of Negative Habits

In our quest for private transformation interior "Simple Ways to Change Your Life in 2024," our interest now shifts to a pivotal thing of increase – the artwork of letting bypass of horrible behavior. Recognizing and liberating the ones conduct is an vital step inside the direction of cultivating a greater healthy, greater exciting lifestyles.

Negative behavior, like subtle shadows, will have a prolonged impact on our lives. In this phase, we are going to shine a moderate on commonplace horrific conduct, unveiling techniques to release their grip and pave the way for remarkable exchange.

Identify Common Negative Habits:

Procrastination: Delaying duties and picks, often leading to improved stress and omitted possibilities.

Negative Self-Talk: Engaging in self-crucial thoughts that undermine self assure and restrict private increase.

Overthinking: Dwelling excessively on beyond activities or annoying approximately the future, primary to anxiety and highbrow fatigue.

Unhealthy Eating Patterns: Consuming immoderate processed factors, sugary snacks, or mindless ingesting as a reaction to strain.

Sedentary Lifestyle: Insufficient physical activity, contributes to fitness troubles and decreased everyday well-being.

Strategies to Overcome and Replace These Habits with Positive Ones

Awareness and Reflection: Identify horrible conduct with the aid of using reflecting on your every day exercises and behaviors. Keep a magazine to tune styles and triggers associated with the ones conduct.

Set Clear Intentions: Define particular, awesome goals to update terrible habits. Focus on the blessings of the first rate changes you cause to advantage.

Gradual Change: Implement modifications step by step to avoid feeling beaten. Break down large goals into smaller, possible steps.

Mindfulness and Meditation: Cultivate mindfulness to emerge as greater aware of your thoughts and behaviors. Incorporate meditation to promote highbrow clarity and emotional stability.

Seek Support: Share your goals with pals or own family for responsibility and encouragement. Consider attempting to find professional guide if wanted, which include a therapist or a life train.

Positive Reinforcement: Celebrate small victories alongside the manner. Reward your self for making brilliant picks and red meat up the brand new conduct.

Replace with Healthy Alternatives: Substitute terrible conduct with more wholesome alternatives. For instance, replace a sedentary dependancy with a every day stroll or transfer unstable snacks with nutritious options.

By identifying, acknowledging, and actively working to replace terrible behavior, you pave the way for a extra extremely good and exciting lifestyles. As you embark on this journey of letting skip, may you discover the power within to cultivate behavior that align collectively together with your aspirations and make a contribution for your commonplace properly-being.

1.Four Cultivating a Positive Attitude

A extraordinary mind-set isn't in reality a nice disposition; it's miles a dynamic force that influences every aspect of our properly-being. In this phase, we are going to treatment the profound impact of positivity and offer actionable tips to nurture and preserve this uplifting mind-set.

Exploring the Impact of Positivity on Overall Well-being:

Emotional Resilience: A high best mind-set serves as a buffer in competition to existence's disturbing situations, fostering emotional resilience and the capability to get higher from setbacks.

Improved Mental Health: Positivity is carefully associated with decrease stages of pressure, anxiety, and melancholy, contributing to a more match intellectual country.

Enhanced Physical Health: Scientific research propose that a effective outlook is associated with better cardiovascular health, improved immune characteristic, and multiplied durability.

Stronger Relationships: Positivity is contagious and fosters harmonious connections. It draws effective energy, enhancing interpersonal dynamics.

Increased Productivity: A fantastic mind-set complements hobby, creativity, and trouble-solving capabilities, major to expanded productiveness in numerous components of existence.

Provide Actionable Tips to Maintain a Positive Attitude:

Practice Gratitude Daily: Begin or stop every day by way of the usage of reflecting on three assets you are thankful for, and cultivate an appreciation for lifestyles's small joys.

Positive Affirmations: Integrate splendid affirmations into your each day everyday, and repeat affirmations that align together with your desires and aspirations.

Surround Yourself with Positivity: Choose to spend time with individuals who radiate positivity, and restriction publicity to horrible impacts, whether in media or personal interactions.

Focus on Solutions: Shift your cognizance from problems to answers, and approach demanding situations with a thoughts-set that seeks boom possibilities.

Mindful Living: Practice mindfulness to stay present and absolutely interact with every 2nd, domesticate popularity of your mind, and redirect horrible styles.

Celebrate Small Wins: Acknowledge and have a laugh your achievements, regardless of how small, create a dependancy of recognizing development and success.

Self-Compassion: Be type to yourself, mainly for the duration of tough times, and deal with your self with the equal compassion you may offer to a friend.

1.Five Setting Realistic Goals

As we delve deeper into the transformative journey cited in " Simple Ways to Change Your Life in 2024," the spotlight now turns to the pivotal idea of placing practical and practicable goals. Goals act as guiding stars, shaping the trajectory of our lives. In this phase, we can find out the profound significance of putting attainable goals and offer a realistic manual to developing SMART desires for the yr in advance.

Discuss the Importance of Setting Achievable Goals:

Direction and Purpose: Setting dreams offers a easy revel in of path and cause, supporting us channel our efforts within the course of huge results.

Motivation and Focus: Well-defined dreams function motivational beacons, supplying a experience of purpose that maintains us centered and decided, even within the course of hard times.

Measurable Progress: Achievable dreams are measurable, allowing us to track development and feature a laugh milestones, reinforcing our determination to the adventure.

Enhanced Decision-Making: Clear goals act as desire-making filters, supporting us prioritize sports activities that align with our objectives and discard distractions.

Increased Resilience: Facing setbacks is inevitable, however well-crafted dreams decorate resilience. They offer a framework for reading from disturbing situations and adjusting our method.

Guide Readers on Creating SMART Goals for 2024:

To set the diploma for a transformative yr, permit's delve into the SMART standards, a strategic framework for crafting dreams which can be Specific, Measurable, Achievable, Relevant, and Time-positive.

Specific: Clearly define your purpose. Be precise approximately what you want to gain.

Instead of a indistinct goal like "exercise extra," specify "stroll half-hour each day."

Measurable: Establish measurable signs and signs and symptoms to tune your improvement. For example, in case your motive is to have a look at greater, set a measurable purpose like "examine one e-book in keeping with month."

Achievable: Ensure that your intention is realistic and viable. Consider your belongings, time, and modern-day commitments. Adjust your reason to align in conjunction with your times.

Relevant: Align your goal together with your broader lifestyles goals. Ask yourself if the purpose is large and contributes for your common properly-being and aspirations.

Time-advantageous: Set a ultimate date for accomplishing your purpose. Adding a time constraint creates a revel in of urgency and enables you stay centered.

Example of a SMART Goal:

Goal: Improve physical fitness in 2024.

SMART Goal: "Engage in 1/2-hour of cardiovascular workout five days in keeping with week for the following six months, to lose five pounds via June."

As you embark on the journey of setting dreams for the approaching year, remember that each cause is a stepping stone in the direction of a more first-class existence. By making them SMART, you empower yourself to show aspirations into tangible achievements.

Here's to a 365 days complete of practical goals and tremendous accomplishments.

Chapter 10: Health And Wellness

Welcome to Chapter 2 of "Simple Ways to Change Your Life in 2024." As we step into the sector of health and well-being, our focus turns to a cornerstone of energy and bodily exercise. Join me in this exploration of the transformative strength of motion and the simplicity of incorporating it into our daily lives.

2.1 Prioritize Physical Exercise

Highlight the Benefits of Regular Exercise and Suggest Easy Ways to Incorporate Physical Activity into Daily Routines:

ReHighlight the Benefits of Regular Exercise and Suggest Easy Ways to Incorporate Physical Activity into Daily Routines:

Regular workout contributes to advanced cardiovascular fitness, bolstered muscles and bones, increased flexibility, and advanced intellectual nicely-being through releasing endorphins — the frame's natural temper lifters, promoting reduced strain, anxiety, and melancholy. It moreover aids in weight control, regulating frame weight for a greater wholesome lifestyle, and boosts power ranges, combating fatigue. Additionally, incorporating exercise is associated with improved sleep first rate, bearing in thoughts deeper, extra restorative rest.

Regular workout contributes to a myriad of health advantages, enhancing each physical and highbrow well-being. It improves cardiovascular fitness, strengthening your coronary heart, lowering the chance of chronic ailments, and boosting typical power. Engaging in everyday bodily hobby moreover strengthens muscle groups and bones, selling higher posture and decreasing the risk of accidents.

Exercise is a effective tool for highbrow nicely-being, because it releases endorphins – the frame's natural temper lifters. This biochemical phenomenon aids in reducing pressure, tension, and despair, growing a pleasant impact for your intellectual nation.

Weight manage is every different extremely good benefit, as incorporating exercising lets in regulate frame weight, fostering a greater in form and extra sustainable way of life.

To resultseasily combine physical interest into day by day carrying activities, recollect starting your day with morning stretches to evoke muscular tissues, utilizing lunch breaks for brisk walks, incorporating diffused desk carrying activities, exploring home bodily sports like yoga or HIIT, lively commuting by the usage of the use of cycling or on foot, sporting out family or pal sports activities like trekking or sports activities, taking component in quick dance breaks for every fun and motion and selecting stairs in place of elevators each time possible. The cause isn't a strenuous fitness journey however to infuse your day with glad motion, whether or now not it's miles a walk, a dance session, or a short home exercising.

To make physical hobby a persevering with a part of your each day routine, endure in mind the following examples:

Morning Stretches: Start your day with a couple of minutes of stretching wearing events. This not simplest wakes up your muscle mass but moreover enhances flexibility, placing a extremely good tone for the day.

Lunchtime Walks: Utilize your lunch damage for a brisk walk around the workplace or close by park. It no longer incredible contributes to bodily health however also offers a intellectual refresh, improving productivity inside the afternoon.

Desk Exercises: Incorporate subtle sports activities at your desk, together with seated leg lifts or neck stretches. These brief carrying occasions fight sedentary artwork behavior, maintaining your body engaged for the duration of the day.

Home Workouts: Explore brief and effective home workout workouts, beginning from yoga to immoderate-intensity c program languageperiod education (HIIT). Online structures offer a number of guided education tailored to exceptional opportunities and fitness degrees.

Active Commuting: If viable, do not forget cycling or taking walks to art work. It's an wonderful manner to sneak in physical activity at the same time as commuting, contributing to every your fitness and the surroundings.

Family or Friend Activities: Plan physical sports activities with loved ones, on the facet of hiking, biking, or playing sports activities collectively. This now not best promotes a healthy life-style however moreover strengthens social bonds.

Dance Breaks: Spice up your ordinary with quick dance breaks. It's a a laugh and energetic manner to transport your frame and uplift your mood, in particular all through paintings breaks or at domestic.

Stair Climbing: Opt for stairs instead of elevators on every occasion viable. This easy but effective preference includes aerobic into your day, constructing cardiovascular health regularly.

Embrace the simplicity of integrating physical exercising into your normal, and can you find out the invigorating effect it has to your body, thoughts, and spirit. Here's to a healthier and similarly colorful you.

2.2 Adopting a Balanced Diet

In the continuing adventure of "Simple Ways to Change Your Life in 2024," our exploration now leads us to a vital hassle of health – adopting a balanced eating regimen. Let's delve into the profound importance of nourishing our bodies with purpose and find out sensible tips for cultivating a healthful and sustainable technique to consuming.

Discussing the Significance of a Balanced and Nutritious Diet

A balanced and nutritious diet is the cornerstone of a wholesome and colourful existence, impacting numerous components of our well-being. Just as a car desires fantastic gasoline to run effectively, our our our bodies require a balanced food plan for top-rated functioning, offering crucial factors desired for energy, boom, and restore. Nutrient-wealthy substances characteristic the gas that powers our physiological techniques, ensuring that our our our bodies function at their brilliant.

Beyond fueling top-excellent functioning, a properly-balanced weight loss program plays a pivotal role in ailment prevention. Rich in nutrients, minerals, and antioxidants, this type of weight-reduction plan acts as a castle, protective the body closer to chronic illnesses, boosting the immune device, and fostering not unusual health. It becomes a proactive diploma, empowering human beings to take fee of their properly-being and decrease the danger of capability fitness troubles.

Weight control is each different key problem recommended by manner of a balanced food regimen. By imparting important nutrients with out excess energy, a balanced weight loss plan facilitates the protection of a wholesome weight. This no longer fine contributes to physical properly-being but also fosters a sustainable and sensible method to weight manage, guidance easy of fad diets and unsustainable practices.

Stable power degrees are a proper away final results of consuming nutrient-dense components. Such food ensure a ordinary release of power, stopping power crashes and promoting sustained cognizance and productiveness inside the route of the day. This issue is vital in navigating the goals of every day existence, whether or now not or now not at art work, in private hobbies, or during enjoyment activities.

The effect of nutrients extends past the bodily realm to intellectual properly-being. A balanced eating regimen facilitates cognitive feature, emotional well-being, and stress manipulate. The elaborate connection amongst vitamins and highbrow health underscores the significance of aware eating and making selections that nourish not handiest the body but additionally the mind.

In embracing a balanced and nutritious eating regimen, human beings domesticate a holistic method to fitness – one that addresses physical, intellectual, and preventive additives. It will become a adventure of self-care and empowerment, wherein the alternatives made at the plate ripple into diverse dimensions of lifestyles. As we discover the importance of a balanced food plan, also can moreover it encourage a dedication to nourishing ourselves in a manner that fosters essential properly-being for the length of each spectrum of our lives.

Offer Practical Tips for Healthy Eating and Cultivating a Sustainable Approach:

In the pursuit of a balanced and nutritious food regimen, sensible hints for healthy consuming characteristic guiding requirements, facilitating conscious alternatives that nourish the frame and sell popular nicely-being. These actionable steps not only enhance the dietary top notch of food however additionally contribute to a sustainable and amusing method to ingesting.

Diversify Your Plate: Aim for a colourful combo of culmination, veggies, lean proteins, complete grains, and healthful fats to your plate. This range ensures a spectrum of nutrients and minerals critical for top-rated health. For example, embody leafy veggies, colourful berries, quinoa, and a deliver of lean protein like grilled hen or tofu.

Mindful Eating: Practice aware ingesting with the useful resource of using savoring every bite. Eating slowly aids digestion and permits your frame to apprehend satiety cues, stopping overconsumption. Eliminate distractions during meals to live attuned in your frame's starvation and fullness signs. Consider incorporating conscious rituals, at the side of expressing gratitude in your meal.

Hydration is Key: Prioritize hydration by way of way of way of making sure an right enough intake of water at some point of the day. Sometimes, emotions of hunger may be a sign of dehydration. Opt for water, natural teas, or infused water to feature flavor with out vain sugars. Create your non-public infused water with slices of cucumber, mint, and citrus give up end result for a easy twist.

Portion Control: Be privy to detail sizes to keep away from overeating. Listen for your body's cues and prevent ingesting while you're happy. This exercising fosters a healthful dating with meals and stops useless calorie consumption. Use smaller plates to visually cue appropriate portions and avoid the temptation to overfill.

Plan and Prepare: Plan your food and snacks beforehand of time to make more healthy choices. Stock your kitchen with nutritious alternatives to reduce reliance on processed or consolation food. Preparation is fundamental to retaining a balanced food regimen amidst a busy manner of life. Consider batch cooking on weekends for quick and healthy food at some level inside the week.

Moderation, Not Deprivation: Embrace a thoughts-set of moderation in vicinity of deprivation. Allowing yourself occasional treats promotes a sustainable approach to eating, retaining off extremes which could result in risky conduct. Consider incorporating a weekly "deal with day" in that you are taking pride in a small part of your preferred dessert or snack.

Read Labels: Familiarize your self with meals labels to make knowledgeable alternatives. Pay hobby to substances, serving sizes, and dietary information. This empowers you to pick out out additives aligned with your health goals. Look for meals with fewer components and lower sugar content fabric material.

Listen to Your Body: Tune into how precise meals make you revel in. Adjust your weight loss program based totally totally on what nourishes and energizes you. This custom designed approach encourages a deeper connection with your body's particular needs. Consider preserving a food magazine to music how unique ingredients effect your power levels, mood, and normal properly-being.

As you embark on the journey of adopting a balanced diet plan, may additionally the ones practical tips come to be partners in your route to joyous and attractive nourishment. Remember, it's far no longer about perfection however approximately cultivating a sustainable and conscious technique to consuming and fostering a way of life that enables your well-being in the long run. May each meal be an opportunity to have a amazing time and honor the top notch relationship among your frame and the nourishing selections you are making.

2.Three Prioritize Mental Health

In the evolving narrative of personal growth, we delve into the sanctuary of the thoughts - highbrow fitness. Explore with me the profound importance of nurturing our highbrow properly-being and discover transformative mindfulness and pressure-remedy techniques.

Addressing the Importance of Mental Well-being and Introducing Mindfulness and Stress-Relief Techniques:

Mental well-being stands because the cornerstone of holistic fitness, exerting a profound have an effect on on our mind, feelings, and moves, in the end shaping each facet of our lives. Recognizing its pivotal function in our not unusual nicely-being is important for fostering a balanced and first-rate lifestyles.

Foundation for Overall Wellness: Mental fitness serves as the foundation for holistic properly-being. It is intricately related with our physical health, influencing our every day alternatives, behaviors, and common extraordinary of life. By prioritizing intellectual well-being, we lay the premise for a greater resilient, realistic, and pleased life.

Resilience inside the Face of Challenges: A sturdy highbrow fitness basis empowers us to face life's worrying conditions with resilience and adaptability. It acts as a shield, supporting us navigate through adversity, setbacks, and uncertainties. Cultivating intellectual resilience turns into a key asset in now not simplest surviving but thriving within the ever-changing landscape of existence.

Enhanced Relationships: The kingdom of our intellectual well-being is intricately woven into the material of our relationships. When we prioritize our highbrow fitness, we contribute to more healthy connections with others. Emotional intelligence, empathy, and powerful verbal exchange are nurtured, developing a fantastic ripple impact that extends to our non-public and professional interactions.

Emotional Balance: A reputation on mental fitness fosters emotional stability, permitting us to govern stress, address adversity, and experience a stronger and extraordinary emotional state. By knowledge and regulating our emotions, we beautify our capability to navigate existence's u.S.A.And downs with grace and resilience.

Introduce Mindfulness and Stress-Relief Techniques

IIn navigating the terrain of highbrow properly-being, the workout of mindfulness and stress-consolation techniques emerges as a guiding light. These intentional practices offer tools to cultivate a tranquil mind amidst the chaos of day by day lifestyles, promoting a experience of internal peace and stability.

Mindfulness Meditation: Engage in mindfulness meditation to supply hobby to the prevailing 2nd, fostering readability of concept and a feel of calm. Dedicate a few minutes every day to take a seat in quiet mirrored photograph, staring at your thoughts with out judgment.

Deep Breathing Exercises: Incorporate deep breathing wearing activities to modify your aggravating tool and sell relaxation. Techniques such as diaphragmatic respiration or area breathing may be with out issues incorporated into your every day recurring.

Mindful Movement: Explore aware motion practices like yoga or tai chi. These sports activities no longer excellent make a contribution to bodily properly-being however moreover domesticate a mind-body connection, fostering a harmonious balance.

Digital Detox: Carve out time for a virtual detox to unplug from the normal flow into of facts. Disconnecting from displays permits your mind to reset and rejuvenate, promoting intellectual clarity and lowering strain.

Remember, prioritizing mental fitness isn't always a luxury but a important issue of a balanced and captivating existence. As you combine mindfulness and strain-relief techniques into your each day normal, May moreover additionally you find out the transformative energy of a nurtured thoughts.

Chapter 11: Personal Growth And Development

Welcome to Chapter 3 of "Simple Ways to Change Your Life in 2024." As we immerse ourselves in the adventure of personal increase and development, this financial ruin unfolds to explore the transformative power of non-forestall gaining knowledge of and the important skills of powerful time management, resilience, networking, and embracing trade.

3.1 Continuous Learning

In the intricate tapestry of lifestyles, each day unfurls as an possibility for profound boom through the pursuit of information. Lifelong gaining knowledge of is not virtually an option; it's a dynamic strain propelling us in the route of self-discovery and success. By embracing a mind-set of non-prevent gaining knowledge of, we adapt, thrive, and make contributions meaningfully to the sector round us.

Embracing Lifelong Learning: The international is an ever-evolving canvas of statistics, and to stay stagnant is to disclaim ourselves the richness that steady mastering brings. Lifelong analyzing is not confined to high school rooms; it's miles an method to life, a philosophy that sees every experience, each assignment, and each interplay as an opportunity to glean insights and increase our expertise.

The Power of Curiosity: At the coronary heart of lifelong analyzing lies an insatiable hobby—a strain that propels us to invite questions, are looking for answers, and venture into uncharted territories of information. It turns the mundane into the fantastic and transforms routine into discovery.

Unveiling New Horizons: In an technology of speedy change, the capability to research constantly will become a superpower. It permits us to comply to the unpredictable, navigate complexities, and loose up new horizons. Lifelong learning is the compass that publications us via the dynamic panorama of private and professional increase.

Beyond Formal Education: While formal education offers a foundation, lifelong gaining knowledge of extends a long way beyond the observe room. It involves devouring books that undertaking our views, carrying out conversations that increase our expertise, and embracing studies that push us out of our consolation zones.

Navigating the Digital Age: The virtual age has bestowed upon us a wealth of statistics at our fingertips. Online courses, podcasts, forums, and documentaries provide avenues for studying that have been as soon as not possible. Embracing technology as a device for continuous gaining knowledge of amplifies our capability to stay knowledgeable and stimulated.

Cultivating a Learning Mindset: To embark in this journey, domesticate a mastering thoughts-set. See setbacks as education, demanding situations as opportunities, and every come upon as a chance to benefit know-how. It's not approximately perfection but about development, no longer approximately expertise the whole thing however approximately being open to reading a few factor.

three.2 Introduction to Effective Time Management:

Time is a finite resource, and the manner we navigate its currents determines the terrific of our days, weeks, and in the end, our lives. Effective time control isn't about squeezing extra duties into each day however about optimizing the usage of our time to align with our priorities and desires.

Understanding Priorities: Before delving into strategies, it's far important to apprehend and apprehend your priorities. What are the goals that rely maximum to you? What obligations make a contribution notably to your personal and expert growth? By clarifying your priorities, you create a roadmap for powerful time allocation.

Techniques for Effective Time Management

The Pomodoro Technique: Break your paintings into durations, traditionally 25 mins in duration, separated via the usage of quick breaks. This permits maintain popularity and stops burnout.

Eisenhower Matrix: Categorize obligations into 4 quadrants based totally on urgency and significance. This matrix aids in prioritization, making sure that essential duties are not overshadowed by using the truly urgent.

Time Blocking: Allocate precise blocks of time to remarkable obligations or types of paintings. This approach enhances reputation thru minimizing multitasking and developing devoted periods for focused strive.

Eat That Frog! (Brian Tracy): Tackle the maximum tough or important mission first element within the morning. This method capitalizes on peak energy degrees and gadgets a top notch tone for the day.

Tools for Prioritization and Productivity

To-Do Lists: Create every day or weekly to-do lists to outline duties and goals. Prioritize those lists based totally on urgency and importance.

Calendar Apps: Utilize digital calendars to schedule appointments, cut-off dates, and obligations. Set reminders to live heading inside the proper route.

Task Management Apps: Explore mission control apps on the way to can help you organize, prioritize, and music your development on severa obligations.

Goal Setting: Establish brief-time period and lengthy-term goals. Break down large goals into smaller, potential obligations with remaining dates.

Cultivating a Productive Mindset: Effective time manipulate isn't certainly approximately outdoor equipment; it is deeply rooted in cultivating a powerful thoughts-set. This consists of recognizing and mitigating time-dropping behavior, fostering region, and getting to know to say no to non-vital commitments.

three.Three Building Resilience:

The Importance of Resilience in Facing Life's Challenges: Life, with its ebbs and flows, is a tapestry woven with moments of pleasure and trials. In the face of adversity, resilience emerges as our steadfast associate, guiding us thru storms and assisting us emerge more potent on the other side. The functionality to get better from setbacks is not best a trait; it's far a dynamic stress that shapes our responses to life's annoying conditions.

Offer Strategies for Developing Resilience:

Cultivate a Positive Mindset: Train your thoughts to cognizance on answers as opposed to residing on issues. Embrace traumatic situations as possibilities for increase.

Build a Support System: Nurture sizeable connections with pals, family, or a resource organisation. Seek and provide help eventually of difficult instances.

Learn from Adversity: View setbacks as reading tales. Extract training from disturbing situations to inform future movements.

Practice Self-Compassion: Treat yourself with kindness throughout difficult instances. Avoid self-grievance and broadly recognized your efforts.

Maintain Flexibility: Develop the ability to comply to changing occasions. Embrace the unexpected with a bendy thoughts-set.

three.Four Networking and Relationship Building:

Discuss the Value of Meaningful Connections: A human connection bureaucracy the fabric of our life, weaving a tapestry of shared research and mutual manual. Meaningful connections now not most effective beautify our well-being but furthermore act as catalysts for increase and opportunity in severa factors of life.

Tips on Building and Maintaining Positive Relationships:

Active Listening: Practice attentive and energetic listening in conversations. And Demonstrate a right interest in others' views.

Authenticity: Be genuine to yourself in relationships. Cultivate authenticity to construct proper connections.

Initiate Networking Opportunities: Attend sports activities or be part of companies aligned in conjunction with your interests. Engage in networking with an open mind and a willingness to connect.

Nurture Reciprocal Relationships: Contribute to relationships with the resource of imparting assist and encouragement. Value and reciprocate the splendid energy within your community.

three.Five Embracing Change:

Embrace Change as a Catalyst for Growth: Change, even though frequently met with resistance, is an inevitable and transformative pressure. Embracing trade permits us to glide with the currents of existence, unlocking doors to new opportunities and private evolution.

Insights into Navigating Transitions:

Cultivate a Growth Mindset: View alternate as an possibility for getting to know and improvement. Embrace demanding situations as stepping stones in the course of personal growth.

Set Realistic Expectations: Understanding that change can also additionally carry uncertainties. Set realistic expectancies and technique transitions with adaptability.

Seek Support: Lean to your assist machine at some stage in instances of change. Share your mind and emotions with trusted buddies or mentors.

Focus on What You Can Control: Identify elements indoors your manipulate at some point of change. Direct your electricity toward tremendous actions internal your sphere of have an effect on.

As we navigate the dynamic panorama of private boom, can also moreover the ones insights into resilience, networking, courting building, and embracing alternate function compass elements, guiding you toward a twelve months of profound transformation and achievement.

Chapter 12: Simplifying And Decluttering

Welcome to Chapter four of "Simple Ways to Change Your Life in 2024." As we step into the serene realm of simplifying and decluttering, be part of me in exploring the profound connection among our surroundings and intellectual well-being. Discover practical steps to declutter every bodily and virtual areas, and embark on a adventure into the world of minimalism, unraveling the splendor of simplicity in our everyday lives

4.1 Decluttering Your Space

As Explain the Connection between Clutters-Free Environment and Mental Well-being: Our out of doors environment mirrors the landscape of our minds. A clutter-loose place isn't always genuinely a polished choice; it is a transformative act that fosters highbrow readability, reduces strain, and complements regular nicely-being. As we declutter our physical surroundings, we create room for tranquility and concept to flourish.

Provide Practical Tips for Decluttering:

Start Small: Begin decluttering one location at a time to avoid feeling beaten. Set viable goals for every decluttering session

Donate or Discard: Assess objects with a vital eye. If some element does now not serve a cause or deliver pleasure, keep in mind donating or discarding it. Create specific boxes for objects to donate, recycle, or throw away.

Organize with Purpose:

AArrange property in a manner that complements capability and accessibility. Invest in garage answers that align together together with your wishes and aesthetic alternatives.

Digital Decluttering: Extend decluttering to virtual regions. Organize documents to your laptop and delete useless files. Clear out unused apps in your gadgets to streamline virtual reviews.

Mindful Consumption: Adopt a conscious technique to new purchases. Consider the software program application and joy a brand new object brings in advance than obtaining it. Embrace a "one in, one out" rule for keeping balance.

four.2 Digital Detox:

Discuss the Importance of a Digital Detox: In the virtual age, our digital areas can turn out to be as cluttered as our bodily environment. A digital detox is a rejuvenating exercising that mitigates data overload, reduces stress, and lets in for added intentional technology use.

Offer Steps to Declutter and Organize Digital Spaces

Evaluate App Usage: Assess the apps to your gadgets. Uninstall or prepare them based on frequency of use. Create folders to group comparable apps for a cleaner home show display display.

Email Organization: Declutter your inbox by way of manner of the usage of unsubscribing from newsletters you now not observe.

Create folders to prepare and categorize emails.

Digital File Cleanup: Regularly review and put together files to your pc. Delete duplicates and antique documents. Utilize cloud storage answers for a streamlined and to be had digital workspace.

Set Boundaries: Establish particular instances for checking emails and social media to avoid constant virtual distractions. Turn off non-vital notifications to create a extra focused digital surroundings.

4.Three Minimalism in Daily Life:

Introduce the Concept of Minimalism: Minimalism is greater than a layout aesthetic; it's miles a way of existence focused spherical intentional dwelling. Embracing minimalism includes simplifying our possessions, that specialize in what truly topics, and fostering a deeper appreciation for the existing second.

Guidance on Simplifying Daily Routines:

Capsule Wardrobe: Curate a pill cloth cloth wardrobe with flexible, essential portions. Reduce desire fatigue and streamline your morning ordinary.

Simplify Meal Planning: Adopt simple and nutritious meal plans to streamline grocery purchasing and cooking. Embrace aware eating with the useful resource of savoring each bite.

Mindful Scheduling: Declutter your calendar thru prioritizing important duties and sports. Create location for rest and amusement to avoid burnout.

Digital Minimalism: Simplify your digital life thru the usage of decreasing show time. Unsubscribe from vain electronic mail lists and limit social media utilization.

As we simplify and declutter, also are we able to discover liberation in letting circulate of excess, cultivating a conscious technique to our environment, and embracing the essence of minimalism in our everyday lives to a life of simplicity, clarity, and intentional living,

Chapter 13: Acts Of Kindness And Volunteerism

Five.1 Acts of Kindness:

Highlight the Impact of Kindness on Personal Well-being: Kindness is a mild strain that not handiest ripples outward, touching the lives of others but additionally flows lower returned, enriching the giver's soul. The act of kindness is not measured thru grand gestures however thru the accumulation of small, intentional acts that create a tapestry of compassion and connection.

Offer Ideas for Incorporating Kindness into Daily Life:

Random Acts of Kindness: Surprise a colleague with a considerate observe or small gift. Pay for someone's coffee or meal in line inside the lower back of you.

Listen with Intent: Practice lively listening in conversations, presenting your entire presence. Be a supply of consolation and useful resource for those going through tough instances.

Extend Help: Offer to assist a person with a challenge or errand, specifically if you apprehend they may be crushed. Volunteer to stroll a neighbor's canine or help with household chores.

Kind Words: Express gratitude and compliments actually. Write notes of appreciation to friends, family, or colleagues.

Empathy in Action: Put yourself in someone else's footwear to recognize their perspective. Offer a comforting presence to the ones experiencing problems.

five.2 Volunteerism:

Discuss the Benefits of Volunteering: Volunteering is a effective catalyst for personal increase and network nicely-being. The act of giving one's time and skills now not handiest contributes to a greater reason but moreover nurtures a sense of reason, connection, and achievement in the volunteer.

Provide Information on Finding Local Volunteer Opportunities:

Community Centers and Nonprofits: Contact nearby community facilities and nonprofit businesses to inquire about volunteer possibilities. Explore roles that align together with your talents, interests, and available time.

Online Platforms: Utilize on line systems like VolunteerMatch (volunteermatch.Org) or Idealist (idealist.Org) to find out network volunteer possibilities. Join community forums or social media groups devoted to shut by using volunteering.

Schools and Religious Institutions: Connect with schools, church homes, or spiritual establishments to find out volunteer responsibilities within the network. Attend community sports to discover approximately ongoing responsibilities.

Corporate Social Responsibility Programs: If hired, inquire about your place of job's agency social duty packages. Participate in commercial enterprise business enterprise-backed volunteer sports activities or recommend new tasks.

Chapter 14: Understanding The Power Of The Subconscious Mind

I received a e-e-e-newsletter one high-quality New Year's morning and that is what it have a look at:

"In my mid-20s, I modified into obsessed on the electricity of the unconscious thoughts.

I examine many books and attended numerous seminars reading how to unleash the power of the subconscious thoughts.

One of the strategies I've placed is to put in writing down my goals.

I did that.

I indexed down the subjects I desired to gain in a notebook. I wrote down how a lot I desired to earn each month, what car I favored to pressure, and what residence I favored to stay in.

After that, I absolutely forgot about it.

Few years later, I located the ebook as soon as I moved residence.

I have become surprised that I had finished all the topics listed in it.

I literally had shivers down my spine once I observed it. I had been my private fortune teller!

Goal writing isn't simplest for making plans, it's far a way to impress upon and have interaction the power of the unconscious mind, which has the functionality to preserve us what we want.

There are a few techniques in purpose writing. They are:

1. Write it in the gift worrying as if you have it proper now. For example, "I earn $10k a month, I stay in a four bed room rental," and so on.

2. The intention you write down ought to resonate with you. If you write 'I earn a million dollars a month' however you can't in reality resonate with it, it's going to simply instill doubt in you.

The language of your unconscious mind is picture and emotion. If you instill doubt, it's going to move again you with doubt.

Give it a strive. Write down the dreams that resonate with you on a bit of paper and preserve it. Then allow skip and paintings in the direction of the goals.

Don't be surprised while it without a doubt works. ;)"

By a long manner this changed into the first-class New Year's e-mail in my inbox. The relaxation have been actually seeking to promote me subjects.

Did you observe the detail in which the letter stated the desires have to resonate with you? What at once got here to thoughts?

It recollect the fundamental purpose why many purpose-setters or New Year decision makers do now not get favorable effects is exactly due to loss of resonation. The way determines the product so in case you don't rent the right method to cause-placing or selection-making, achievement will elude you.

"Dream Big!" Motivational speakers say, and that they're now not incorrect. But there may be an unwritten rule that your desires and desires aren't alleged to exceed your not unusual kingdom or electricity stage. If you've ever recorded failure within the actualization of your desires, you want to ask yourself some vital questions.

First, did you convert them into SMART goals or did you honestly reflect onconsideration on in your head with out making any actionable plans? Even in case you wrote them for your magazine or planner, you'd despite the fact that need to break them down. It's not truly "make extra cash this 12 months" but "open store half of-hour earlier to lure the early chook clients" if you're a roadside food supplier.

It is actual that the more focused you are in breaking down and spelling out how you're going to collect your dreams, the much more likely you're to be triumphant.

The wrong approach to intention-putting might have been your purpose for the horrible results or failure ultimate year however no longer anymore.

If you haven't sorted the resonation factor of your cause-setting kindly offer hobby to it.

Resonation is the issue in which you try and win yourself over so you can effectively engage the electricity of the subconscious mind, and direct it inside the course of your goal. In different phrases, write down what you want and make your self receive as real with it.

This might be very important to avoid doubt. Doubt can jeopardize the fulfillment of your dreams. You're likely familiar with the word "beyond all lower priced doubt;" if you should ruin your dreams then you definately without a doubt in reality have to region it past the gain of doubt in any other case, doubt will harm it for you.

At this juncture, it is probably top notch to understand precisely how doubt operates, but first permit me let you know a tale:

Did you recognize tha in 1994, Jeff Bezos, a then 30-yr-vintage hedge fund manager, turn out to be seeking out funding for a modern idea: a web e-book shop. To recognize this vision, Bezos launched into a quest to steady investments of about $50,000 every from functionality investors, normally targeting own family contributors, pals, and others who is probably willing to take a threat on his concept. According to statistics assets, Bezos's adventure to raise rate variety for his nascent company emerge as no small feat. He held 60 meetings, tirelessly pitching his idea to influence others of its capability. Despite his efforts, he confronted severa rejections. Out of the 60 human beings he approached, nice 22 have been satisfied to spend money on his idea, contributing to the $1 million he had to begin Amazon.Com Inc. In usual, he gave up 20% to early customers, in keeping with a 2013 article on Geekwire.

Back in 1994, the net changed into a long way from mainstream, and loads of had been skeptical approximately its capacity. This skepticism end up pondered inside the reactions of capacity traders. As Bezos recalled, "The first query people had, have emerge as what modified into the internet?" He stated that everyone with expertise of the e-book industrial employer did no longer invest, illustrating the challenge of convincing humans to spend money on an unusual and unproven concept.

Today the relaxation is statistics as Amazon is considered one of the most important businesses in the worldwide.

Doubt emerges while topics do no longer degree up, surely as we observed with 38 of the humans Jeff Bezos pitched his online business concept. Jeff's Idea didn't add as much as them just so they walked out and lost big time.

Let's say you wrote for your pocket ebook: 'I make $1million monthly' and it does now not resonate with you as it's too much then reduce it. If but, what you wrote down is what you stubbornly want, even without you seeing a way you may gain it by using the moves you've written down, then it's the time to set up blind faith. This form of faith is not virtually blind but furthermore stubborn, and a number of human beings were capable of have interaction their subconscious minds with it. They have, over the years, been linked inexplicably with the right contacts who've helped them make that dream a truth.

So whichever preference you pick out, your dreams should resonate with you to be effective in attractive the electricity of the subconscious thoughts.

Another element that assist you to harness the power of the subconscious mind is the solution to this question: "What is that large difficulty you desire to do after you have turn out to be a success at attaining your goals?" This is wherein the feelings are available to enhance your why. For instance, after you've got got performed your reason of $1million a month, you will be capable of arrange loose food for a large sort of destitute human beings on a every day basis. You should even sponsor unfastened healthcare and feeding for street dogs and other strays. Or you is probably able to keep the coral reefs on the sea ground in Hawaii, which researchers say has depleted by way of the use of over 50% thinking about the truth that over-tourism took over the stunning Islands.

What I am pronouncing basically is that during case your preference to acquire your goals is simply strong, if you've been mad or emotionally hyped over that one trouble, you then definately truly have more than enough passion to interact the energy of the unconscious thoughts, and function it artwork in the direction of the success of that purpose.

The description above is specially at the way to get your desires to resonate with you, however that's virtually the number one detail.

The 2nd detail is likewise critical due to the fact, for every desired very last results, a demand is positioned on you. Based on that call for there need to be a few sort of adjustable planning so that you can stay resilient within the path of the running and ready period. For instance, if your purpose is an earnings of $1 million monthly, you could multiply it via 12 to mirror the sum in a 365 days, that's $12 million.

Next, take that bulk sum ($12 million) and destroy it down into one year, fifty weeks, and 366 days. This will task the quantity you want to be making in step with week and consistent with day.

Now to devise for the danger that the plan may not workout consultation precisely inside its predetermined time body of twelve months, ruin the majority sum into eleven months, 48 weeks, and 336 days. Then on a separate net internet page harm it down all over again into 10 months, 44 weeks, and 306 days. Follow the identical machine and smash your proposed bulk sum into, nine months, eight months, 7 months, 6 months, 5 months, four months, and ultimately 3 months.

3 months is the minimal because of the fact a few trouble it's far you need to do, you need time to do it. Three months is the least feasible time from what I've placed but as an alternative miracles do rise up. The motive for all this breaking down is that, the clearer your reason is the better you may resonate. A sturdy resonation manner the energy of the unconscious mind has been engaged.

Now do the equal with the achievability or the to-do segment. Set SMART dreams regular with each time allotment. The cause for this adjustable planning is to preserve you inspired all the manner for upwards of 9 months right away. A notable feat truely. This is also in agreement with the Self-determination concept or SDT.

This idea proposes that humans have a critical want for independence, competence, and relatedness. Therefore feeling like we've got choices and manipulate over our choices fulfills our want for independence and may truly effect our motivation, engagement, and delight.

In unique phrases, the options are there because it feels amazing to have options. This will preserve your enthusiasm tiers up even even as you do now not meet your dreams each day in a month or every month in a 12 months. It'll moreover maintain up your Will to achieve success because of the reality that each one you need to do is optimize your try to boom productivity and ensure that you meet the ones dreams via the forestall of the twelve months.

Chapter 15: The Influence Of The Subconscious Mind On Our Behavior

The subconscious thoughts are the part of our highbrow hobby that operates underneath the quantity of aware recognition. It plays a essential function in shaping thoughts, behaviors, and consequences by means of influencing preference-making, feelings, and perceptions without our specific consciousness. The subconscious thoughts stores reminiscences, beliefs, and reviews, contributing to conduct and automated responses. Understanding and coping with the subconscious can motive top notch adjustments in a unmarried's mind-set and moves.

The unconscious thoughts strategies and shops information through a complicated network of neural connections. Experiences, recollections, and emotions are encoded inside the mind, forming a reservoir of knowledge that impacts behavior. Beliefs are regularly ingrained in the subconscious thru repetition, emotional establishments, or high-quality lifestyles events.

Memory consolidation includes moving quick-term reminiscences to lengthy-term storage inside the mind, where the subconscious mind can get right of access to them. Emotions are related to testimonies and are saved alongside related memories. Positive or horrible emotional institutions can shape future reactions and choice-making.

Beliefs end up embedded within the unconscious via ordinary reinforcement, whether or not from personal opinions, societal impacts, or repeated exposure to positive thoughts. The unconscious thoughts tends to really be given statistics without crucial evaluation, making it liable to outside impacts.

Overall, the unconscious thoughts competencies as a reservoir of collected experiences, feelings, and ideals, shaping our perceptions and influencing our mind and moves on a unconscious level.

How the subconscious mind affects day by day moves: Examples of the manner beliefs saved within the subconscious have an impact on behavior.

The unconscious thoughts significantly influences each day moves through the use of influencing conduct in strategies frequently not noted thru the conscious mind. Beliefs stored in the subconscious can shape reactions, choices, and conduct. Here are examples of the way subconscious ideals have an effect on conduct:

Self-esteem and Confidence: If a person holds unconscious beliefs of low self confidence, they could constantly undermine their very very own competencies, keeping off traumatic situations and restricting personal growth.

Fear and Anxiety Responses: Past worrying reviews saved in the unconscious can purpose fear or anxiety responses in situations corresponding to those beyond sports activities, affecting choice-making and emotional well-being.

Habits and Addictions: Subconscious ideals about coping mechanisms or self-soothing can lead to the improvement of behavior or addictions. For example, a person with a notion that smoking relieves stress might also conflict to stop because of the unconscious affiliation.

Relationship Patterns: Unconscious beliefs about receive as authentic with, vulnerability, or worthiness could have an effect on relationship dynamics. Patterns of behavior, collectively with avoiding intimacy or suffering with dedication may additionally additionally furthermore stem from deeply rooted ideals.

Success and Failure Mindset: Subconscious ideals approximately one's capacity for fulfillment or failure can impact profession choices and achievements. A man or woman with a belief in their abilities may additionally moreover pursue bold goals, at the identical time as a person with deep-seated doubt also can hesitate to take dangers.

Perception of Challenges: The manner annoying situations are perceived is regularly precipitated via unconscious beliefs. A person with a boom attitude may moreover view disturbing situations as possibilities to research, whilst someone with a hard and fast mindset also can see them as insurmountable obstacles.

Understanding and addressing these subconscious ideals can be vital for non-public development. Techniques like mindfulness, treatment, and fantastic affirmations can help reshape and reprogram the unconscious mind, fostering more powerful and optimistic behaviors.

Introduction to strategies for attractive the transformative force of the subconscious: Discussions on visualization, high-quality affirmations, and exclusive sensible techniques.

Engaging the transformative pressure of the subconscious includes the usage of severa strategies to reshape ideals and effect conduct. Here are a few practical methods:

Visualization: Picture favored consequences in your thoughts. Vividly believe achieving goals, whether or not or now not it is profession achievement, superior relationships, or personal boom. Visualization lets in align the subconscious thoughts with great visions, reinforcing a sense of possibility.

Positive Affirmations: Repeat effective statements that reflect the changes you need to look to your life. Affirmations artwork through regularly changing terrible or limiting beliefs with greater empowering ones, influencing the subconscious mind over the years.

Mindfulness and Meditation: Practices that inspire present-moment interest can assist calm the mind and permit for a greater deliberate affect on the subconscious. Mindfulness and meditation offer a region to check mind without judgment and make intentional changes.

Hypnosis: Guided hypnosis lessons can get right of entry to the unconscious directly, selling relaxation and receptivity to tremendous pointers. Professional hypnotherapy or self-hypnosis recordings may be effective device for transformative alternate.

Reframing Negative Thoughts: Actively assignment and reframe horrible mind. When a negative belief arises, consciously update it with a excessive great and optimistic counterpart. Consistent strive can little by little shift unconscious styles.

Journaling: Writing about tales, feelings, and preferred modifications can supply unconscious mind to the floor. Regular journaling affords perception into underlying ideals and allows for intentional redirection of idea patterns.

Gratitude Practice: Cultivate a habit of expressing gratitude every day. Focusing on first-rate components of lifestyles can shift the unconscious in the direction of a more constructive mindset, influencing primary well-being.

Behavioral Exposure: Gradually reveal yourself to conditions that task limiting beliefs. Facing fears or doubts in a managed manner can assist rewire the unconscious by way of way of growing new, fine associations.

Remember, consistency is top when running with the subconscious. These techniques are pleasant at the same time as practiced regularly over the years, allowing the unconscious mind to mix and adopt the preferred changes.

The connection some of the subconscious mind and physical properly-being: Highlighting research or examples showcasing the mind's impact on fitness.

The connection among the unconscious mind and bodily well-being is a well-mounted issue, regularly called psychosomatic medicinal drug. Numerous studies and examples illustrate how intellectual and emotional states impact physical health:

Placebo and Nocebo Effects: Research continuously demonstrates the energy of notion in shaping fitness results. Placebo effects, in which humans enjoy enhancements due to the perception in a treatment, highlight the have an effect on of the mind at the body. Conversely, the nocebo impact, in which lousy expectations result in volatile outcomes, emphasizes the effect of terrible ideals on fitness.

Stress and Immune Function: Chronic stress has been associated with weakened immune function. The unconscious mind's response to stress, along with persistent negative thoughts or unresolved trauma, can make a contribution to the release of pressure hormones, affecting the frame's functionality to shield in competition to ailments.

Mind-Body Interventions: Practices like meditation, mindfulness, and guided imagery have established amazing results on bodily fitness. Studies mean that those interventions can lessen pressure, lower blood pressure, and decorate commonplace properly-being through undoubtedly influencing the unconscious mind.

Psychological Resilience and Recovery: Individuals with robust intellectual resilience regularly get better extra correctly from contamination or surgical procedure. The subconscious thoughts, with its characteristic in coping mechanisms and notion structures, plays a important position in resilience and may impact the fee and effectiveness of healing.

Chronic Pain and Emotional Factors: Chronic ache situations regularly include a complicated interplay of bodily and emotional elements. The unconscious thoughts can make a contribution to the belief and manage of pain. Cognitive-behavioral recovery strategies, which deal with concept styles and beliefs, have examined powerful in handling chronic pain.

Mind-Body Connection in Chronic Diseases: Conditions which embody irritable bowel syndrome (IBS), fibromyalgia, and autoimmune disorders are increasingly identified as having strong thoughts-body connections. Stress, tension, and emotional nicely-being play awesome roles in the onset and exacerbation of these situations.

Mindfulness-Based Stress Reduction (MBSR): Programs like MBSR had been related to improvements in severa fitness conditions, which incorporates chronic ache, cardiovascular health, and intellectual health. These interventions art work by using manner of the use of fostering attention of thoughts and feelings, influencing the unconscious thoughts's effect on bodily fitness.

These examples underscore the intricate relationship some of the unconscious mind and physical properly-being. Integrating intellectual and emotional fitness into basic fitness strategies is crucial for holistic properly-being.

Chapter 16: The Placebo Effect In Healing

In severa clinical research, patients have professional incredible recoveries in truth with the aid of believing they have been receiving an powerful treatment, even if given a placebo. These instances spotlight the profound effect the unconscious mind should have on the body's capability to heal. Realizing the potential of the mind in influencing health has delivered approximately extended exploration of mind-frame connections in scientific practices.

Norman Cousins' Laughter Therapy:

Norman Cousins, an American journalist, confronted a excessive infection that left him in constant ache. Determined to get higher, he integrated laughter into his recovery technique. He watched funny movies and engaged in sports that added him pride. Cousins believed that great emotions can also additionally need to motive the release of restoration chemical substances inside the body. Over time, his fitness improved considerably, and his story have end up a testomony to the role of a superb thoughts-set in overcoming infection.

Louise Hay's Positive Affirmations:

Louise Hay, a motivational writer, emphasized the connection amongst mind and bodily health. After being recognized with most cancers, she incorporated superb affirmations and visualization into her every day ordinary. Louise attributed her recovery to the energy of changing her subconscious beliefs about herself and her frame. Her journey have become an inspiration for hundreds seeking out holistic strategies to fitness.

Jim Carrey's Visualization and Goal Setting:

Before accomplishing fame, actor Jim Carrey wrote himself a test for $10 million for "acting offerings rendered" and dated it for five years within the future. He visualized himself receiving this type of sum for his acting roles. Remarkably, Carrey finished this economic milestone inside the precise time frame. His tale exemplifies the impact of visualization and perception in shaping one's reality.

These memories illustrate how humans have harnessed the transformative capability of the unconscious thoughts to conquer stressful conditions, advantage goals, and enjoy profound recuperation. They emphasize the importance of mind-set, beliefs, and emotions in influencing the direction of one's existence.

Strategies for identifying and overcoming proscribing ideals to encourage you to undertaking and reshape bad concept styles.

Identifying and overcoming limiting beliefs is a important step closer to personal growth. Here are techniques that will help you apprehend and alternate the ones horrible belief styles:

Self-Reflection:

Regularly introspect for your mind and emotions. Identify normal styles and be privy to situations that cause self-doubt or negativity. Awareness is the first step in tough restricting beliefs.

Question Your Beliefs:

Actively query the validity of your beliefs. Ask your self if they are based totally on information or assumptions. Challenge the evidence helping lousy thoughts and keep in mind opportunity, more empowering perspectives.

Keep a Thought Journal:

Record your thoughts in a journal. Document conditions that evoke sturdy emotions and the related ideals. Analyzing those entries through the years can display screen patterns and provide insights into your subconscious attitude.

Seek Feedback:

Reach out to relied on friends, own family, or mentors for feedback in your ideals. Others might also furthermore offer precious views and help you notice elements of your self that you could now not be conscious.

Mindfulness Practices:

Engage in mindfulness meditation or practices that sell present-2d attention. Mindfulness enables you've got a take a look at mind without judgment, making it easier to understand and venture restricting beliefs.

Positive Affirmations:

Replace horrible self-talk with high terrific affirmations. Create and repeat statements that counteract restricting beliefs. Consistency is high in reshaping concept styles over the years.

Visualization:

Picture your self succeeding in situations in that you commonly doubt your competencies. Visualization can assist reprogram your unconscious thoughts thru growing high-quality highbrow pictures and institutions.

Set Realistic Goals:

Break down massive goals into smaller, workable steps. Success in these smaller duties can mission the notion which you are incapable or unworthy, gradually building self belief.

Explore Root Causes:

Examine the origins of your restricting ideals. Understand inside the event that they stem from adolescence memories, societal expectations, or past failures. Addressing the idea causes permits for added effective transformation.

Challenge the "Shoulds" and "Musts":

Be aware of self-imposed expectations that begin with "I should" or "I must." Evaluate if the ones expectations align along with your proper values and within the occasion that they contribute surely to your life.

Remember, overcoming proscribing beliefs is an ongoing manner. Be affected person with yourself and have a good time small victories alongside the way. By actively hard and reshaping terrible concept patterns, you could foster a mind-set that permits non-public increase and well-being.

The function of mindfulness and meditation in tapping into the subconscious mind and the way those practices can enhance self-hobby and transformation.

Mindfulness and meditation play a tremendous feature in tapping into the unconscious mind, fostering self-interest, and promoting personal transformation. Here's how those practices make a contribution to a deeper understanding of the unconscious:

Present-Moment Awareness:

Mindfulness encourages attention to the present second with out judgment. By being simply gift, people can test their thoughts, emotions, and sensations, gaining perception into the workings of their subconscious mind.

Observing Thoughts and Emotions:

Meditation cultivates the potential to observe thoughts and emotions without attachment. This detachment allows individuals to witness the content in their subconscious mind objectively, fostering a deeper knowledge of ordinary idea styles.

Quieting the Mind:

Through meditation, the thoughts step by step quiets down, reducing the normal chatter of mind. In this stillness, human beings can get right of access to deeper layers of recognition, revealing underlying beliefs and feelings that might not be right now obvious in every day life.

Stress Reduction:

Mindfulness and meditation are powerful in reducing stress, which has a right away impact on the subconscious mind. As strain diminishes, the mind becomes extra receptive to splendid changes, facilitating a greater open and adaptable unconscious state.

Enhanced Self-Awareness:

By constantly practicing mindfulness, human beings boom heightened self-cognizance. This self-attention extends to the subtle components of the unconscious, deliberating the popularity of automated thoughts, proscribing ideals, and emotional reactions.

Cultivating Mindfulness in Daily Activities:

Mindfulness isn't always restricted to formal meditation periods. Integrating mindfulness into daily sports, which includes ingesting, strolling, or maybe going for walks, permits people to maintain a kingdom of heightened recognition, influencing the subconscious mind in the path of the day.

Embracing Non-Judgment:

Mindfulness encourages a non-judgmental attitude closer to one's mind and emotions. This recognition creates a compassionate area for exploring the unconscious without self-criticism, facilitating a greater high-quality technique to non-public transformation.

Connecting with Inner Wisdom:

Through mindfulness and meditation, humans frequently document a deeper reference to their internal know-how or intuition. This connection can offer precious insights into subconscious ideals, guiding the procedure of transformation inside the path of more aligned and actual living.

Mind-Body Connection:

These practices emphasize the mind-body connection, acknowledging that highbrow and emotional states impact physical well-being. As humans end up more attuned to this connection, they are able to cope with subconscious styles that may be affecting their standard fitness.

In essence, mindfulness and meditation act as effective gadget for exploring the unconscious thoughts, fostering self-recognition, and promoting transformation. Practice this regularly to create a intellectual surroundings conducive to wonderful exchange, allowing you to navigate the depths of your subconscious with readability and reason.

Chapter 17: Practical Guides For Visualization Exercises

Visualization is a effective tool for tapping into the subconscious mind. Here are realistic physical video games to guide readers in harnessing the power of visualization:

Create a Relaxing Environment:

Find quiet and comfortable vicinity in that you may not be disturbed. Sit or lie down in a relaxed role. Close your eyes and take some deep breaths to center yourself.

Visualize Your Ideal Day:

Envision your best day from start to complete. Picture yourself waking up feeling energized, venture fun sports activities, and challenge your goals. Pay hobby to details, colorings, and feelings associated with every scenario.

Future Self Visualization:

Imagine your destiny self, finished and content. Picture the achievements you choice and the man or woman you want to turn out to be. Visualize the self belief, joy, and achievement that accompany your destiny success.

Goal Achievement Visualization:

Choose a particular aim you are running within the route of. Close your eyes and vividly accept as true with your self reaching that goal. Feel the emotions associated with success, whether or not it's miles satisfaction, happiness, or a enjoy of accomplishment.

Mind-Body Healing Visualization:

Focus on an area of your body that may need restoration or rejuvenation. Visualize a circulate of healing mild or strength flowing into that area. Imagine it repairing and restoring, selling standard nicely-being.

Create a Vision Board:

Compile images and terms that constitute your goals and aspirations. Arrange them on a imaginative and prescient board, a physical or digital university. Spend time often looking at your vision board, allowing the photographs to rouse powerful emotions and toughen your unconscious beliefs.

Guided Meditation for Visualization:

Use guided meditation recordings or apps that lead you via visualization bodily games. These frequently embody turns on that will help you believe particular situations, fostering a deeper connection with your subconscious mind.

Positive Affirmation Visualization:

Pair powerful affirmations with visualization. Choose affirmations that align together collectively along with your desires or preferred thoughts-set. As you repeat the affirmations, visualize them coming to existence, reinforcing the high-quality ideals related to them.

Morning Routine Visualization:

Incorporate visualization into your morning habitual. Take a couple of minutes each morning to visualise a a success and splendid day beforehand. Set the tone in your day by using specializing in intentions and preferred consequences.

Reflect and Adjust:

After each visualization session, take a 2d to mirror at the emotions and insights that arose. Adjust your visualizations as needed to align in conjunction with your evolving dreams and aspirations.

Why now not make visualization a ordinary workout, preferably incorporating it into your each day regular? Consistency is top, as normal visualization lets in improve excessive extremely good beliefs, reshape concept patterns, and installation a extra empowering attitude over time.

Scientific Research and Findings on the Power of the Subconscious Mind

While medical studies at the subconscious mind are large, incorporating unique studies into a conversation may be difficult because of the format. However, I can offer preferred references to remarkable research regions helping the impact of the unconscious thoughts:

Placebo and Nocebo Effects:

Numerous studies, inclusive of these achieved thru Benedetti and Colloca, spotlight the placebo effect's actual effect on ache treatment and symptom improvement. These findings emphasize how beliefs and expectancies, frequently rooted in the unconscious, have an effect on physiological responses.

Mindfulness and Brain Changes:

Research through manner of Holzel et al. And Davidson et al. Exhibit structural modifications in the thoughts associated with mindfulness practices. These modifications encompass changes within the amygdala, a area associated with emotional processing, suggesting that mindfulness may want to have an effect on the mind's reaction to feelings.

Cognitive-Behavioral Therapy (CBT) for Limiting Beliefs:

Studies, alongside side the ones reviewed through Butler et al., constantly show the effectiveness of cognitive-behavioral treatment in addressing proscribing beliefs and reshaping concept patterns. CBT interventions goal unconscious cognitive procedures, ensuing in notable behavioral outcomes.

Visualization and Motor Cortex Activation:

Research through Mulder et al. Shows that intellectual practice consultation and visualization can prompt the equal neural pathways as physical practice. This supports the concept that visualizing desired consequences engages the unconscious mind and can decorate performance.

Mind-Body Interventions and Gene Expression:

Studies, like those through using Bhasin et al., recommend that thoughts-frame interventions, which incorporates meditation, can have an effect on gene expression related to strain response and contamination. These findings provide scientific insight into how intellectual states effect physical fitness at a molecular stage.

While the ones references provide a glimpse into the scientific exploration of the subconscious thoughts, it's miles critical to be aware that the arena is continuously evolving. Readers interested in a deeper know-how can explore these particular studies and related literature for a more entire view of the scientific proof helping the mind said.

In summary, we've delved into the charming realm of the unconscious thoughts, exploring its complex workings and the profound effect it has on our thoughts, behaviors, and common well-being.

The subconscious mind is a rich reservoir of untapped ability. By expertise its have an effect on, wearing out sensible physical sports, and leveraging scientific insights, readers can embark on a journey of self-discovery and transformation. The key lies in the consistent utility of these thoughts, permitting the unconscious thoughts to come to be a powerful great pal in shaping a greater intentional and empowered existence.

How to Become a More Consistent Person

Becoming a extra regular person consists of growing conduct and techniques that promote reliability and stability to your movements. Here are some thoughts to help you domesticate extra consistency:

Set Clear Goals:

Define your quick-term and prolonged-term goals. Having a easy imaginative and prescient of what you need to acquire presents motivation and direction, making it much less complex to live consistent.

Prioritize Tasks:

Identify your maximum critical obligations and prioritize them. Focus on finishing immoderate-precedence objects in advance than transferring directly to a whole lot much less important sports activities sports. This allows keep consistency in tackling critical responsibilities.

Establish Routine:

Create a each day or weekly recurring that includes genuine instances for art work, self-care, and special priorities. Consistent sporting events help build conduct and make it much less tough to stay on course.

Break Down Goals:

Divide big dreams into smaller, possible duties. This technique makes it less overwhelming and allows you to attain development continuously, reinforcing high-quality behavior.

Accountability Partners:

Share your desires with a friend, member of the family, or colleague who can serve as an duty companion. Regular check-ins and discussions approximately progress can assist keep you accountable.

Create Reminders:

Use device like calendars, venture manage apps, or reminders in your cellular phone to prompt you about responsibilities and commitments. Regular reminders help consistency through maintaining you on time table.

Practice Self-Discipline:

Cultivate energy of mind via focusing at the prolonged-term advantages of your movements. Remind yourself why consistency is essential for attaining your desires and retaining excessive nice conduct.

www.ingramcontent.com/pod-product-compliance
Lightning Source LLC
Chambersburg PA
CBHW071440080526
44587CB00014B/1926